The Decoys

Other books by Bernard Edwards

Masters Next to God
They Sank the Red Dragon
The Fighting Tramps
The Grey Widow Maker
Blood and Bushido
SOS – Men Against the Sea
Salvo!
*Attack and Sink**
*Dönitz and the Wolf Packs**
Return of the Coffin Ships
*Beware Raiders!**
*The Road to Russia**
*The Quiet Heroes**
*The Twilight of the U-boats**
Beware the Grey Widow Maker
*Death in the Doldrums**
*Japan's Blitzkrieg**
*War of the U-boats**
*Royal Navy Versus the Slave Traders**
*The Cruel Sea Retold**
*War Under the Red Ensign 1914–1918**
*The Wolf Packs Gather**
*Convoy Will Scatter**

*Titles in print with Pen & Sword Books.

The Decoys

A Tale of Three Atlantic Convoys, 1942

Bernard Edwards

Pen & Sword
MARITIME

First published in Great Britain in 2016 by
PEN & SWORD MARITIME
an imprint of
Pen & Sword Books Ltd
47 Church Street
Barnsley
South Yorkshire
S70 2AS

ISBN 978-1-47388-708-4

Typeset by Concept, Huddersfield HD4 5JL.
Printed and bound in England by CPI Group (UK) Ltd, Croydon CR0 4YY.

Pen & Sword Books Ltd incorporates the imprints of Pen & Sword Archaeology,
Atlas, Aviation, Battleground, Discovery, Family History, History, Maritime,
Military, Naval, Politics, Railways, Select, Social History, Transport, True Crime,
and Claymore Press, Frontline Books, Leo Cooper, Praetorian Press,
Remember When, Seaforth Publishing and Wharncliffe.

For a complete list of Pen & Sword titles please contact
PEN & SWORD BOOKS LIMITED
47 Church Street, Barnsley, South Yorkshire, S70 2AS, England
E-mail: enquiries@pen-and-sword.co.uk
Website: www.pen-and-sword.co.uk

Contents

List of Plates

Foreword

The real heroes of the Battle of the Atlantic were the officers and men of the Merchant Service; everyone who served at sea knows that. Even the name 'Merchant Service' was a misnomer; these men served in no organized force, wore no uniforms, earned no recognition or awards. They were civilians, and although they earned a far higher rate of pay than any naval man, no wage scale could possibly have recompensed them for the hardihood and endurance which kept them at sea, in helpless and often inadequate ships, in defiance of the terrors of the wartime North Atlantic.

Lieutenant James Barrett Lamb, RCNVR
HMCS *Camrose*

Introduction

Operation Torch, the Allied invasion of French North Africa, was a product of Russian insistence, American impatience, and British compromise.

In the spring of 1942, Hitler's Panzers, striking deep in to the heart of Soviet Russia, were within 100 miles of the gates of Moscow, and Stalin's demands for the opening of a second front in Europe were becoming more and more strident. This, coming from a man who, when Britain stood alone and under threat of invasion, had signed a non-aggression pact with Hitler and supplied Germany with war materials, was the height of hypocrisy. Even so, in order to preserve the alliance between the three nations, it was imperative that something was done to placate the Russian dictator.

The American generals took up the challenge with characteristic gung-ho, proposing an all-out assault on the beaches of northern France there and then. Had they but paused to analyse the prevailing situation, they might have been less eager. American forces were then fully occupied with the Japanese in the Far East, and Britain was heavily engaged with Rommel's Afrika Corps in the Western Desert. Operation Sledgehammer, as the Americans optimistically code-named it, was, for the time being at least, clearly out of the question.

Pragmatic as ever, Winston Churchill proposed a compromise, but first the enemy's defences must be tested. He later wrote in his memoirs:

> I thought it most important that a large scale operation should take place this summer and military opinion seemed unanimous that until an operation on that scale was undertaken, no responsible general would take the responsibility of planning the main invasion.

And so, Operation Jubilee was born.

Jubilee, which took place on 19 August 1942, was an Allied attack on the German occupied port of Dieppe involving 5,000 men of the

2nd Canadian Infantry Division, 1,000 British Commandos and 50 United States Rangers. Ships of the Royal Navy transported the troops, and the RAF gave air cover. The objective of the operation was not to gain a foothold in Europe, but to test German resistance and to seize and hold Dieppe for a few hours. Then, before being evacuated, the troops were to create as much havoc as possible by destroying coastal defences and port installations.

The raid turned out to be a complete disaster for the Allies. Coming under heavy German fire, the landing force failed to get off the beaches and, ten hours after first setting foot onshore, was forced to evacuate, leaving behind more than 3,000 men killed, wounded, or taken prisoner. The Royal Navy lost a destroyer and 33 landing craft, and 106 RAF planes were shot down. The Germans, on the other hand, suffered only 311 killed and 280 wounded, while the *Luftwaffe* lost forty-eight aircraft.

In the light of the dismal failure of Operation Jubilee, which at such terrible cost had proved his point, Churchill put forward an alternative plan to invade North Africa; to 'strike at the soft underbelly of Europe', as he put it, beginning with landings in Morocco and Algeria, both of which were known to be weakly garrisoned by the Vichy French. The Battle of Alamein had been fought and won and Montgomery's Eighth Army had Rommel on the retreat. If, Churchill reasoned, the Germans and Italians, squeezed between Montgomery and Allied troops advancing from the west, were forced out of North Africa, landings on Sicily, and the Italian mainland, would be possible. Side by side, the British and Americans would then fight their way up the spine of Italy into Europe. The plan made immediate sense to President Roosevelt and, eventually, to his generals.

Operation Torch was timed to begin at dawn on 8 November, with simultaneous landings by Allied forces at Casablanca on the Atlantic coast, and Oran and Algiers in the Mediterranean. The plan called for a series of convoys, carrying 70,000 men and their equipment, to sail from British and American ports. A total of 600 ships would be involved, 350 of them crossing the Atlantic from the USA, and 250 from British ports sailing south to Gibraltar. The US Navy would provide cover for the transatlantic convoys, while 160 British escorts were to be withdrawn from other areas, mainly from the North Atlantic trade convoys, to protect the southbound force. This was at a time when Dönitz had at his disposal 330 U-boats, of which at least 140 were at sea and operational on any given day, and the gap in air cover between Newfoundland and Iceland – the *Black Pit*, as it was so aptly named by those who sailed through it – was 600 miles wide. Given that the North Atlantic convoys were already poorly defended, and losing up to 100 ships a month, any further withdrawal of over-worked destroyers and corvettes from northern waters could prove catastrophic. But Torch was considered of such importance that all other considerations must come second.

While preparations for Operation Torch went ahead, German Intelligence was completely unaware that anything of this magnitude was afoot. This was quite out of character for the usually highly efficient *B-Dienst*, and while Hitler and his generals slept soundly, their enemies were plotting revenge for past defeats. In the broad waters of Chesapeake Bay, in the upper reaches of the River Clyde, and in British ports further south, the invasion forces were massing. High-sided troopships, deep-laden supply vessels, fleet tankers, and warships of every size and description were crowding the anchorages. The torch would soon be lit.

It is now known that before Torch began, Dönitz had received advance warning of the sailing of three convoys supposedly unconnected with the operation, RB 1 and SC 107 eastbound across the North Atlantic, and SL 125 northbound from Freetown. These convoys were poorly defended and, unaware of the momentous events taking place elsewhere, Dönitz threw the full weight of his U-boat arm against them. While the U-boats were thus occupied, the huge armada of ships on passage to the beachheads of North Africa slipped past unseen. Not one shot came their way, not one single ship was sunk.

There can be no doubt that the presence of RB 1, SC 107 and SL 125 in the North Atlantic was largely responsible for saving Operation Torch from turning into a complete fiasco. If the U-boats had not been fully involved with them, it was inevitable that the troop convoys would have been seen and attacked. Was it just luck that saved Torch, or were, as has been speculated, RB 1, SC 107 and SL 125 used as decoys, baited hooks, to draw the U-boats away? Whatever the truth, the sacrifice these convoys made in ships and men was appalling, and their story is worth the telling.

CHAPTER ONE

Operation Maniac

It was high summer on the Firth of Clyde, August 1942, and the pristine waters that once hosted threshing paddle steamers filled with excited day trippers were all but deserted. The pleasure boats were long gone, swallowed up by the Admiralty's hungry maw, and spewed out again as gun-toting minesweepers. In their place, a few grey-painted merchantmen came and went about their wartime business, joining convoys, leaving convoys, some of the latter bearing the scars of battle and heading for the repair yards of the Upper Clyde. They all gave way as a great liner glided majestically downstream, her three tall funnels trailing smoke and brightly coloured code flags snapping at her yard arms. Even in her sombre coat of Admiralty Grey, the *Queen Mary* was an impressive sight.

Current holder of the coveted Atlantic Blue Riband, with a top speed of 31 knots, the 81,000-ton RMS *Queen Mary* was the fastest merchantman afloat. She had once carried the cream of Europe and America's aristocracy in her luxurious cabins, but now, stripped down to the bare essentials for trooping, she was ferrying 3,000 service personnel and civilians across the Atlantic to the great powerhouse of the West. Among her passengers were 550 Merchant Navy officers and men, volunteer crews for ships waiting on the other side.

Recruited by Coast Lines of Liverpool acting for the Ministry of War Transport, the merchant seamen were under the impression that they would be joining newly-built ships, replacements being turned out by American shipyards to compensate for the enormous losses to the U-boats' torpedoes then being suffered by Britain. It was perhaps just as well that these eager volunteers had no inkling of the bizarre adventure on which they were soon to embark.

The five-day transatlantic passage passed without incident, the *Queen Mary*, accompanied by a British anti-aircraft cruiser, steaming at full speed. She berthed in New York, where the volunteers spent two blissful weeks enjoying all the delights that were in such short supply in wartime Britain. And while they were wined and dined by the generous New Yorkers, their ships were being made ready for the coming voyage.

Soon after America was drawn into the war in December 1941, the US War Shipping Administration requisitioned eleven lake and river passenger steamers for use by the US Navy. In July 1942, they were transferred to the British Ministry of War Transport under the Lease-Lend Agreement, and placed under the management of Coast Lines of Liverpool. Manned by British crews and flying the Red Ensign, they were to cross the Atlantic and, so it was rumoured, be used as hospital and accommodation ships. They were as follows:

The *Boston* and *New York*, identical steam passenger ships of 4,989 gross tons. Built in 1924 and owned by the Eastern Steamship Lines of Boston, Massachusetts, they were employed on an over-night service between Boston and New York, via the Cape Cod Canal. In reality, they were 'make-believe' passenger liners, much favoured by honeymoon couples and tourists. Their shallow draught and high unprotected sides made them totally unsuited for ocean voyaging.

The 1,978-ton *Naushon* and 1,116-ton *New Bedford* of the New England Steamship Company, built in 1928 for ferry service between the mainland and off-lying islands of Martha's Vineyard and Nantucket Island, and never intended to stray out of sight of land. The same applied to the Chesapeake Bay ferries *Northland* and *Southland* owned by the Norfolk & Washington Steamboat Company. Built in 1911, they were slightly larger at 2,055 and 2,081 tons respectively, again shallow draught vessels designed for sheltered waters. The 1,547-ton *Yorktown* of the Chesapeake Steamship Company of Baltimore had been similarly occupied. So had the 1,814-ton *President Warfield*, built in 1928 for the Baltimore Steam Packet Company to operate an overnight service between Baltimore and Norfolk.

The 2,158-ton *Virginia Lee*, built in 1928 for the Pennsylvania Railroad Company for service as a ferry in Chesapeake Bay. She was described by Royal Navy Signalman Barry Ainsworth, who served briefly in her, as 'something straight out of *Showboat*, it had about six decks, ornamental wooden rails and a stove-pipe funnel – the only thing lacking was a rear paddle wheel'.

The *Colonel J.A. Moss*, of 842 tons, built in 1925 for the Steamer Belle Isle Company as an excursion steamer on the lower Hudson.

The *John Cadwalader* of the Baltimore & Philadelphia Steamboat Company, a ship of 1,478 tons built in 1926 for service in Chesapeake Bay.

The three last mentioned ships were withdrawn before sailing, the *John Cadwalader* becoming a total loss when she went on fire at Philadelphia on 29 August, while the *Virginia Lee* and the *Colonel J.A. Moss* were, very wisely, considered unsuitable to attempt the Atlantic crossing. The eight remaining, namely, *Boston, Naushon, New Bedford, New York, Northland, President Warfield, Southland* and *Virginia Lee*, were then made ready for sea. Their lower decks were filled with empty 40-gallon drums and their open sides boarded up with heavy timbers, while each ship was armed with a 12-pounder HA/LA gun, four 20mm Oerlikons, four parachute and cable (PAC) rockets, and a .303 calibre Ross rifle. The latter, a favourite with the Royal Canadian Mounted Police at the turn of the century, was a long-barrelled rifle with incredible accuracy, presumably to be used for sinking floating mines.

The eight ships chosen to cross the North Atlantic ended up, intentionally or not, looking remarkably like ocean-going passenger liners. In truth, they were nothing of the sort. They were still shallow draught, almost flat-bottomed, inland waterway pleasure steamers. Billy Wells, a greaser in the engine room of the *Boston*, wrote in a letter home: 'We are sailing home in an orange box with an engine, not seaworthy to sail on a park lake, let alone the Atlantic Ocean.' First Radio Officer Tony Slevin was even more derogatory when he first saw his ship, the *Southland*: 'With her whaleback bows and high superstructure I would not have been surprised to see a paddle wheel at the stern. Coal was dumped on deck as the bunkers were too small … After two years at sea, I was seasick. *Southland*, nearly 40 years old and used to the *Delaware*, didn't like it either I suspect.'

Convoy RB 1, code named Operation Maniac, sailed from St John's, Newfoundland on the afternoon of Monday, 21 September 1942, and formed up into four columns for the ocean passage. Captain Robert Young, commanding the *Boston*, had been appointed as convoy commodore, and was leading Column 2, the second column from port. The vice-commodore was Captain Chilion Mayers, in the *New York*, at the head of the outer port column. Appropriately, the 1,116-ton *New Bedford*, late of the New England Steamship Company, was appointed as rescue ship, and took station astern of the *Boston*. The ex-inter-island ferry had a good turn of speed and a low freeboard, but was not otherwise equipped for rescue work.

Once clear of the harbour, the convoy was joined by its ocean escort, which comprised the two V and W-class destroyers HMS *Vanoc* and *Veteran* – both were relics from an earlier war, 25 years old, but still warships to be reckoned with, having a top speed in excess of 30 knots, and armed with quick-firing 4-inch guns, torpedo tubes, and an ample supply of depth charges. The Senior Officer Escort (SOE), Acting Commander Charles Churchill, RN, was in *Vanoc*, while *Veteran* was commanded by Lieutenant Commander Trevor Garwood, RN.

The weather at the time of sailing was fair, except for the long Atlantic swell, which rarely subsided. The high-sided merchantmen, unaccustomed to the movement of the open ocean, did not take kindly to the swell, developing a top-heavy roll, hardly welcomed by their crews, who had been too long on dry land. The rolling also revealed that the ships' magnetic compasses, not having been corrected and compensated for those waters, were seriously inaccurate.

Heinz Walkerling's first war patrol in command had not yet proved to be the war-changing adventure he had anticipated. The 27-year-old kapitänleutnant had commissioned the Type VIIC U-91 in Lübeck at the end of January 1942, and after three months working up in the Baltic, sailed from Kiel on 15 August. All had gone well at first, U-91 sailing the length of the North Sea undetected, entering the North Atlantic through the gap between Iceland and the Faroes on the last day of August. And there Walkerling's run of good luck ran out.

On 1 September, U-91 was motoring on the surface when an American Catalina flying boat came over the horizon flying low, and bracketed the U-boat with depth bombs before she was able to dive. The U-boat sustained superficial damage, but by the time the Catalina had banked and returned for a second attack Walkerling had cleared the conning tower and taken her down. When the second stick of bombs fell, U-91 was too deep for them to have any affect.

Ten days later, when in mid-Atlantic, and having had no other contact with the enemy, U-91 was ordered to join Group *Vörwarts* (Forward) in an attack on the westbound convoy ON 127. In a running battle that continued for five days, U-91 was damaged by gunfire from the escorts and was forced to retreat.

On the 23rd, U-91, sailing in company with U-380, which had also been damaged in the fracas with ON 127, sighted a small convoy about 400 miles east of St John's. Walkerling reported it as a fast convoy on a course of 060°, and steaming at 10–11 knots, with some of the ships resembling passenger liners. This led Admiral Dönitz to the conclusion that it was a 'special troop convoy' and he ordered U-91 and U-380 to shadow. Meanwhile, he called in Group *Blitz* (Lightning), five boats which were then 700 miles to the north-east.

A report by Leading Seaman Jim Read, serving aboard HMS *Vanoc*, explains why Dönitz identified RB 1 as a troop convoy:

> To the seasoned crews of convoy escorts of all types of cargo and troop transports, the eight ships of RB 1 presented something we had not seen before, not cargo ships, but ships of a high super-structure, two with twin funnels and others with high single funnels. From a distance, in a haze or at night, a U-boat periscope just above sea level could quite easily recognise these ships as large troopships, some resembling our more famous liners.

Forty-eight hours out of St John's, zigzagging in daylight and steering a straight course at night to lessen the risk of collision, RB 1 made steady progress to the north-east. The weather continued fair, with a light to moderate breeze and excellent visibility. In more peaceable times this would have been considered a bonus for the North Atlantic, but the older hands in the ships argued that the customary howling gale and driving rain was a far better defence against prowling U-boats. And that those U-boats were already snapping at their heels became evident as the day drew to a close.

At about 1800, just as the sun was setting, COMINCH, the office of the C-in-C of the US Navy, signalled to the SOE in HMS *Vanoc:*

> URGENT U-BOAT WARNING. A U-BOAT ESTIMATED YOUR AREA BY DF AT 2002Z/23 HAS MADE A SIGHTING REPORT OF CONVOY OR IMPORTANT UNIT.

The warning was passed to the Convoy Commodore in the *Boston*, who signalled by flag to all ships: 'SUBMARINES IN VICINITY'.

There was little sleep for anyone in the night that followed. Guns were manned, lookouts doubled, and no man strayed far without his lifejacket to hand. Then, as dawn broke on the 24th, Commander Churchill sent the following signal to the C-in-C Western Approaches:

> RB 1 WAS SHADOWED FROM AHEAD ALL LAST NIGHT AND SUSPECT SHADOWING CONTINUES TODAY THURSDAY 24TH. ESCORTS HAVE INSUFFICIENT FUEL TO CARRY

OUT PUTTING DOWN SWEEP. EVASIVE TACTICS PROVED
USELESS IN EXTREME VISIBILITY WITH FULL MOON. AIR
COVER WOULD BE APPRECIATED AS SOON AS POSSIBLE.
53 14 N 35 20 W COURSE 074, 12 KNOTS.

The warnings were coming in thick and fast now, both COMINCH
and the Admiralty monitoring and pin-pointing by DF the flurry of
radio messages passing between the gathering U-boats. In fact, a total
of seventeen U-boats were either in contact with the convoy or closing
in. However, the day passed without an attack developing. Then, late
that afternoon, the Admiralty warned *Vanoc* to expect an attack during
the night. The message was passed to all ships by lamp from the
Boston's bridge.

By the time darkness came, the whole of the convoy was on full
alert, with all eyes searching the horizon, and Asdics pinging and
radars probing in the escorts, while all guns were loaded and fully
manned. Yet, as the hours ticked by, all remained quiet. By midnight,
the stress of waiting for the attack to materialize was becoming intoler-
able. Finally, at about 0200 on the morning of the 25th, the U-boats
made their move.

In close touch with the convoy were U-91, U-96, U-211, U-260,
U-380, U-404, U-410, U-584 and U-607, and one by one they made their
roll of the dice, but thanks to the magnificent defence put up by the
destroyers *Vanoc* and *Veteran*, they all failed in their objectives. The
entry in Admiral Dönitz's War Diary describes the action:

> U91 was forced to submerge and lost contact. U96 and U380
> were not able to haul ahead of the fast convoy because of engine
> trouble.
> U584 was forced away by a destroyer. U260 lost contact after an
> unsuccessful attack.
> U211 fired a double miss at a 2-funnelled steamer.
> U410 was forced away by a destroyer.
> U607 made an underwater attack and was picked up and
> rammed by a destroyer. Depth charges were dropped.
> These reports show how very difficult it is to get ahead because
> of the enemy's high speed. When submarines are forced to sub-
> merge by destroyers, contact is lost. Boats formerly belonging to
> Group Blitz and Pfeil which are stalking the convoy from the
> northeast have no speed restriction after the morning of 24.9.

While there is no mention made in British reports of U-607 being rammed, there can be no doubt that *Vanoc* and *Veteran* were fully occupied that night in fending off the attacking U-boats, much of the time at high speed. Inevitably, a great deal of fuel was consumed. Each destroyer carried 374 tons of fuel oil when fully bunkered, more than ample for an Atlantic crossing at 12–15 knots, but when manoeuvring at speed, their 27,000 shaft horsepower turbines consumed oil at an alarming rate. With no means of refuelling at sea, Commander Churchill grew more and more concerned as the night went on.

Dawn came on the 25th, and Convoy RB 1, now steaming in a single line abreast, was still intact. After the trouncing they had received in the night, the U-boats appeared to have pulled back, and during the morning there was an opportunity for hot food to be passed around, and even time for desperately tired men to snatch an hour's sleep. But this was only the calm before the storm returned with renewed intensity.

Second Officer Thomas Cottam, serving in the *Northland*, years later wrote down his recollections:

> I took over the 12.00–4.00pm watch at noon and was concerned about the enormous error in the compass, Captain Becket having given me the ship's noon position. As the sun was shining for the first time since leaving Baltimore I was determined to get an azimuth. Mounting the ladder up to the bearing compass, over my shoulder I noticed a hoist of flags going up from the Commodore's ship the *Boston*. I made my way down to read the hoist through the ship's telescope. With the flags in focus, suddenly they all disappeared and in their place was a great column of smoke and flame and then I heard an almighty explosion.

U-216 was a relative newcomer to Group *Blitz*. Commissioned in Kiel by 28-year-old Oberleutnant Karl-Otto Schultz, she had first joined Group *Lohs* in a mid-Atlantic attack on the westbound convoy ONS 122, but had come away empty-handed, which was perhaps foreseeable. She was a Type VIID boat, one of six of a kind built primarily for minelaying, and not really suited to convoy attack work. Her main weakness was that she had a top speed on the surface of only 16½ knots, as compared with the 18 knots of the Type VIIC.

When U-216 made contact with Convoy RB 1, she had been at sea for over a month, and still had not opened her score against the enemy.

Then, when on the afternoon of 25 September Karl-Otto Schultz saw the twin-funnelled, high-sided *Boston*, he knew his luck had changed at last. Seen through the lens of the periscope, she had the appearance of a large passenger liner which, after consulting his ship identification books, Schultz decided was of the 'Viceroy of India type', and probably packed with American troops on their way to Britain. Taking careful aim, he fired a spread of four from his bow tubes.

U-216, the slow, unwieldy minelayer, had vindicated herself. Two of Schultz's torpedoes found their target in the *Boston*, one in her engine room and one in her bow. The ageing ex-pleasure steamer capsized, and went down in seven minutes, but not before Captain Young and his entire crew of sixty-five had abandoned ship in four lifeboats and two rafts, this despite the heavy swell running.

The appointed rescue ship *New Bedford*, stationed outside and astern of the *Boston*, immediately moved in to pick up survivors, but she soon showed how unsuited she was to the task in hand. A heavy wooden fender, a relic of her days as a ferry, ran the length of her hull on both sides, just above the waterline, and when she lowered a boat to pick up the men on the rafts, the boat caught under this and capsized. Fortunately, HMS *Veteran* had by this time arrived on the scene, and rescued Captain Young, forty-six of the *Boston*'s crew, plus Chief Officer Kaye of the *New Bedford*, who had ended up in the water when her boat capsized.

Captain J. Beckett, commanding the ex-Chesapeake Bay overnight ferry *Northland*, described the action in his report to the Admiralty:

> I assumed the submarine had come from the port side and was in between the two port columns. I put my helm to port in case there should be another enemy submarine on the port side, thereby reducing the target. We fired a few rounds in the direction of where I thought the submarine was and then I could see the rear ship in the outside port column, *New Bedford*, which had been appointed rescue ship at a conference held before we left, proceeding to pick up survivors from the torpedoed ship. I turned completely round, fell out of line of the convoy and went to see if I could be of any assistance, but did not bring any survivors on board. Four lifeboats were seen to be got away from the *Boston* but from what I gathered from one of the survivors later only two of the crew of the Commodore ship went on board the rescue ship, the remainder appeared to prefer to go over to one of the

destroyers, their reason being that it was an easier ship to board than the rescue ship . . . In the meantime, the destroyers had closed in and the *Vanoc* signalled me to rejoin the convoy.

When I had got within 3 miles of the convoy – I had left the *Vanoc* and the *New Bedford* astern of me – a submarine was seen to surface some 1,500 yards from my port bow, at about 2045Z on 25 September. We were then in position 54° 36' N 26° 18' W. It appeared to be about a 740-ton vessel, rusty in colour – no doubt from long service, and from the silhouettes we were shown I should say it was a U-37. We immediately opened fire with our Oerlikon and 12 pdr. I had Army gunners manning the Oerlikons and the Naval gunners on the 12 pdr, and the corporal in charge of the Oerlikons opened fire first giving a lead to the 12 pdr crew. It is my opinion that the naval ratings did not see the submarine until the Oerlikon guns went into action and from my position on the bridge I definitely saw the tracers from one of the Oerlikons enter the enemy amidships on the third burst, although the first and second rounds fell short. The submarine crash dived as a result of being hit.

Captain Williams, of the *Northland*'s sister ferry *Southland*, had a similar experience:

. . . I sighted the periscope of a submarine 200–300 yards off our starboard beam. I immediately swung the ship round to bring it astern and carried on on a zig-zag of my own, going hard to starboard and then to port. Speed was increased to 13 knots, but as this was forcing the ship, our maximum speed being 12½ knots, steam naturally fell and we got back to normal. The other vessels also increased speed but the formation and station keeping of the convoy was not good. We opened fire with our 12 pdr and got away fourteen rounds after which we lost sight of the enemy. I did not see the submarine again but shortly after we ceased firing the gunners saw a periscope appear on the port quarter. Eighteen more rounds were fired when the enemy disappeared from view and was not seen again. Whether it was the same submarine or not I am unable to say. The firing of our 12 pdr was very very rapid and I remarked afterwards that I had never seen anything quite so rapid before. Although the first shots fired were wide, the others did not seem to be far away from the target.

The convoy was now scattered over a wide area, both escorts and the rescue ship *New Bedford* being some miles astern rescuing survivors from the torpedoed *Boston*. Also missing was the *New Bedford's* ex-stable mate *Naushon*. As a result of violent evasive action taken when the U-boats attacked, her helm had jammed hard over, and for a while she steamed around in circles while her engineers struggled to repair her steering gear. When the *Naushon* did finally resume her course, the main body of the convoy was all but out of sight.

Darkness had fallen before the convoy was reformed, the seven remaining merchantmen being in single line abreast, the *New York* having been appointed as commodore ship in place of the *Boston*. The two destroyers were guarding the flanks, *Veteran* to port and *Vanoc* to starboard. Convoy speed was set at 9 knots, with the ships zigzagging around a mean course of 080°. Then, as some of the ships were having difficulty in keeping up, the Acting Commodore, Captain Chilion Mayers, in the *New York*, reduced speed to 7 knots. This, although necessary, unfortunately gave the U-boats, then also scattered, an opportunity to close in.

U-96, a Type VIIC under the command of the young Oberleutnant Hans-Jürgen Hellriegel, opened the next phase of the attack. As might be expected, Hellriegel set his sights on the largest target visible, the 4989-ton, twin-funnelled *New York*. At 2057, Hellriegel fired a spread of two from his bow tubes at what he had identified as a 17,000-ton passenger vessel of the *Reina del Pacifico* type. Both torpedoes found their mark, and the *New York* caught fire and dropped out of the convoy. Captain Mayers and his crew of sixty-seven abandoned ship, and for the second time in eight hours RB 1 lost its commodore ship. The *New York*, her built-up wooden sides burning fiercely, remained afloat for another hour, before U-91 found her, and despatched her with another three torpedoes.

The torpedoing of the *New York* led to confusion and the eventual complete break-up of the convoy. Second Officer Cottam, who was on the bridge of the *Northland* when Hans-Jürgen Hellriegel's torpedoes stopped the *New York* in her tracks, wrote of the reaction aboard his ship:

> At this point the chief engineer hove into the wheelhouse and demanded if we were going to remain like a sitting duck and be blown out of the water. Captain Beckett said, 'Give me the steam and we'll make a run for it.'

Captain Beckett's call for more steam was granted in full, and the *Northland* parted company with the convoy, working up to 16 knots as her sweating firemen hurled coal into her roaring boiler furnaces. Adopting an improvized zigzag, Beckett pulled away to the north, anxious to escape the clutches of the voracious pack of U-boats intent on savaging the convoy. And as the *Northland* disappeared into the darkness of the night, others followed suit. Soon, Convoy RB 1 had ceased to exist.

The SOE, Commander Churchill, in HMS *Vanoc*, sent HMS *Veteran* in pursuit of the vanishing ships, but she searched in vain. She did, however, come across two lifeboats with seventy-eight survivors from the torpedoed ships *Boston* and *New York*. Shortly after dawn on the 26th, she stopped to take these men on board, it being fully light by the time this was completed. As she got under way again to rejoin *Vanoc*, her Asdic operators picked a firm echo, and Lieutenant Commander Garwood raced in to attack with depth charges. He was too late. Otto von Bulow, in U-404, who had been watching the rescue operation at periscope depth, fired a spread of three torpedoes.

Two of Von Bulow's torpedoes hit the *Veteran*, one of them penetrating her main magazine, causing a massive explosion that literally blew her apart. Lieutenant Commander Garwood, his entire crew of 159, and the seventy-eight men who minutes before had been giving thanks for their deliverance, all disappeared with the destroyer. When a search was made for the missing *Veteran*, no wreckage, no bodies, not even a slick of oil was found.

Of RB 1's merchant ships, the *Northland*, *Southland*, *New Bedford*, *Naushon* and *President Warfield* all reached port safely. Only the ex-Chesapeake Bay ferry *Yorktown* came to grief, and this when she was only thirty-six hours steaming from the sanctuary of the North Channel.

Captain Boylan reported to the Admiralty:

Everything went well until 2200 GMT (2050 Convoy Time) on 26 September when in position 55° 10' N 18° 50' W we were struck by a torpedo on the port side immediately under the bridge. The sea at the time was very rough with a high swell and wind WNW force 6, the sky was overcast and visibility was about 2 miles ... we were proceeding at 12½ knots on a course of 081° (true).

I was in my room lying down and everything collapsed around me and I had great difficulty in struggling out through the mass of debris. When I got on deck I found that all the superstructure forward of the bridge, which was made of wood, had collapsed, including the bridge. The engine had stopped immediately and very soon after I reached the deck the ship began to crack and rend which I thought was No. 2 bulkhead giving way. The ship sank within about 3 minutes.

The *Yorktown* had been unfortunate enough to cross paths with U-619, one of the Group *Blitz* boats that had not previously been able to make contact with Convoy RB 1. Oberleutnant Kurt Makowski thus sank the second ship of his short career, which ended ten days later south-west of Iceland, when U-619 was sunk with all hands by a patrolling British aircraft.

Despite the rough weather, and the fact that the *Yorktown* went down so quickly that there was no time to get the boats away, only eighteen of her crew of sixty-two were lost. Even so, this took the total of lives lost from this small but bizarre convoy to a staggering 302 – and for what gain? Berlin certainly thought the U-boats' torpedoes had been well spent, describing RB 1 as a convoy of large troopships, and falsely identified three of the ships lost as the *Viceroy of India* (19,648 tons), *Reina del Pacifico* (17,702 tons) and the *Derbyshire* (11,660 tons).

Convoy RB 1 is an enigma that to this day remains unsolved. The reason given for bringing these eight ageing, flat-bottomed lake steamers across an ocean crawling with U-boats in the approach to winter was that they were urgently needed as accommodation ships for the projected invasion of France. As D-Day was then nearly two years away, the urgency of the need must be questioned. The five ships that survived the Atlantic crossing were converted into accommodation or hospital ships, and some did eventually cross the Channel in 1944, but for the most part they spent the rest of the war laid up in the backwaters of the south of England.

CHAPTER TWO

Prelude to Torch

The West African port of Freetown is no tropical paradise. Tropical it may be, but it is a far cry from the idyllic *get away from it all* destination of the travel brochures. In the wet season, the heat is unbearable and the rain falls incessantly; in the dry months it is just hot and damp. Little wonder that in the 1940s, with preventative medicine still in its infancy, Freetown's cemeteries were full of the graves of intrepid colonialists who had succumbed to the regions epidemic fevers.

It was in early October 1942, at the height of the wet season, that Convoy SL 125 lay at anchor in Freetown's deep-water anchorage. They had come from far and wide, thirty-seven merchantmen with cargoes from the Indian Ocean, South America, and Africa itself, all bound for United Kingdom ports. The ships were largely British, with a sprinkling of Norwegian, Dutch, Belgian, Swedish, and one lone American freighter. Many of them had been swinging to their anchor for weeks while the convoy gathered, but even the late comers were anxious to see the back of this African sweatbox to which the war had brought them.

An almost audible sigh of relief echoed around the anchorage when, on the morning of 16 October, flags raced up the halyards and signal lamps began to flash and, with a great hissing of steam windlasses and clanking of chains, anchors were brought home. The sun was well up behind the heavy clouds when the long line of ships filed out of Freetown harbour. In the lead as the convoy moved out through the buoyed channel and edged past the old wreck on Carpenter Rock was British India's 5,283-ton *Nagpore*, assigned as commodore ship for the passage home. Commanded by Captain Percy Tonkin, and with the convoy commodore Rear Admiral Sir Cecil Reyne on board, the *Nagpore* was from the East with 7,000 tons of general and 1,500 tons of copper in her holds.

Once clear of the land, Convoy SL 125 formed up in eleven columns abreast and was joined by its ocean escort, which consisted of the four Flower class corvettes *Cowslip*, *Crocus*, *Petunia* and *Woodruff*, with the SOE, Lieutenant Commander John Rayner, in HMS *Petunia*. The spectacle of the four diminutive warships bravely attempting to form a protective screen around them did little to inspire confidence in those who were about to challenge Dönitz's U-boats. Their vulnerability was brought home to them when, shortly after forming up, a signal was received from the Admiralty reporting that the 20,000-ton troopship *Oronsay* had been torpedoed and sunk some 150 miles from Freetown. It was perhaps just as well that no one was then aware that German naval intelligence, *B-Dienst*, had already decrypted a message giving full details of SL 125, including its course and speed. As the mountains of Sierra Leone dropped astern of the convoy, Admiral Dönitz was already calling in his grey wolves to set up an ambush near the island of Madeira.

In direct contrast to Freetown, New York in the late autumn of 1942 was that Utopian world at the end of the rainbow. America had been at war for almost a year, but apart for the multitude of uniforms on show, there was little outward sign of conflict in the great city. At night, the lights still shone as bright as ever, rationing was something which happened only on the far side of the Atlantic, and the bars and restaurants of Times Square reverberated to the 'big band' sound.

Down on the Manhattan waterfront, the scene was nearer to reality, grey-painted freighters lined the wharves with tall dockside cranes weaving and dipping over their open hatchways. Tanks, guns, jeeps, pallets of K-rations, and all the other necessities of war were being loaded into the cavernous holds of the waiting ships with a sense of urgency rarely seen on the New York dockside. Tongues wagged, as they always will, and the informed consensus of opinion was that 'something big' was on. The pundits were not wrong. As October drew to a close, Operation Torch was about to get under way.

Torch was timed to begin at dawn on 8 November, with an all-American landing of 35,000 troops on the beaches near Casablanca on Morocco's Atlantic coast. At the same time another American force, 18,500 strong, would land at Oran, and 20,000 British and American troops would go ashore near Algiers. There were known to be about 120,000 Vichy French troops in Morocco and Algeria, but no German or Italian forces, so little resistance was anticipated.

The planning for Torch was meticulous, with secrecy paramount. Seven convoys, carrying the 73,500 men and their equipment, were to sail from British and American ports, the first being scheduled to leave Chesapeake Bay for Casablanca on 19 October. It was estimated that overall at least 600 ships would be used in the operation, and this was at a time when the number of U-boats in the Atlantic had never been greater. Huge risks were involved.

The first Torch troop convoy from the USA, code-named UGF 1, bound for the landing beaches near Casablanca, began to assemble in the shelter of Hampton Roads in mid-October, and was ready to sail by the 24th of the month. It then consisted of thirty-six large merchantmen, carrying General George Patton's 35,000-strong Western Task Force, and finally sailed on the 26th. Filing past Cape Henlopen in single line abreast, the ships entered the open Atlantic and formed up into nine columns abreast. The manoeuvre took much of the day, and night was falling before course was set to the east. UGF 1 was then joined by its covering force of three battleships, three heavy cruisers, four light cruisers, three escort carriers, one seaplane tender, three minesweepers and forty-three destroyers, along with the 1,235-ton salvage tug *Cherokee II*, which presumably was there to deal with any unforeseen casualties through adverse weather or enemy action. Overhead, US Army Air Force planes patrolled in strength, and would do so until they ran out of range. In overall command of the convoy was Rear Admiral Kent Hewith in his flagship the heavy cruiser USS *Augusta*. This whole huge assembly of ships, covering the ocean as far as the eye could see, appeared impregnable, and was certainly the most heavily defended body of ships ever to set out across the Atlantic. The Americans were not about to risk their ships or their men on the long ocean crossing.

Contrast the departure of Convoy SC 107, which was at the same time sailing from New York. This was also a convoy off to war. In the holds of its ships, which once carried tea from India, wool from Australia, and beef from Argentina, were the tanks, guns, aircraft and vehicles, the accoutrements of battle needed for Operation Torch. The majority of the merchantmen also carried substantial quantities of ammunition and high explosives, the foremost candidate for a quick trip to oblivion being British India's *Hatimura*. In addition to a cargo of 8,200 tons of war materials she carried in her 'tween decks was 200 tons of TNT, 250 tons of gunpowder and 300 tons of incendiaries. In the event of being torpedoed, it seemed highly unlikely that any of the *Hatimura*'s crew would survive, but no one on board seemed to give much thought to such a morbid prospect. They might be living on top of a floating bomb and about to cross the most dangerous stretch of ocean in the world, yet to them all that mattered was that they were homeward bound.

Leading the ships as they passed the Ambrose Light vessel and entered deep water was the 5,318-ton British steamer *Jeypore* under the command of 39-year-old Captain Tom Stevens. She carried the convoy commodore ex-Vice Admiral RN, now Commodore RNR, Bertram Watson, whose role it would be to play shepherd to the multi-flagged collection of merchantmen as they ran the gauntlet of the U-boats in the Atlantic. Commodore Watson, aged 55, who retired from the Navy in May 1940, had seen service in the First World War as Navigating Officer with the Harwich Force. Along with several hundred retired senior officers of his ilk, he had returned to the Navy in the lower rank to apply his considerable knowledge to convoy work.

The *Jeypore*, built in the Sunderland yard of William Gray for the Peninsular & Oriental Steamship Company, was in her twenty-second year at sea and far from her usual trading waters. Sailing under the house flag of the British India Company, a subsidiary of P&O, she had spent most of her life in the East, where her officers dressed in smart tropical uniforms, and awnings were stretched for long lazy days spent in port. The war had put a sudden end to those idyllic times. Now, painted drab grey and salt-stained, the *Jeypore* was loaded to her winter marks with 6,200 tons of military cargo, including an uncomfortably large quantity of ammunition, and about to challenge the angry North Atlantic.

When assembled, Convoy SC 107 consisted of twenty-five merchant ships. They were joined at first light on the 24th by their escort, led by the British destroyer *Wanderer*, with the Canadian destroyer *Columbia*, the corvette HMCS *Kamsack*, and the minesweeper HMCS *Trois Rivieres*. Bringing up the rear of the convoy was the British rescue ship *Stockport* and two New York harbour tugs. Requisitioned by the US Navy, the 250-ton *Pessacus* with a crew of ten, and the slightly larger *Uncas* with a fifteen-man crew, were on passage to Iceland. In addition to the dangers they faced from the weather, the tugs had been detailed to assist the *Stockport* with picking up survivors in the event of an attack.

In the early days of the war, little consideration was given to convoy rescue work. It was left to the rear ships to rescue survivors on an *ad hoc* basis, but as stopping to lower boats carried a high risk of the rescuer being torpedoed, few masters were willing to participate. All too often, it fell to the escorts to carry out this work, and while they were so engaged they were unable to protect the convoy, which was, after all, their primary role.

At the beginning of 1941, the first dedicated convoy rescue ships were brought into service. Small merchant ships with a good turn of speed and some passenger accommodation were called for, and none were more ideal than the cross-channel ferries, which by virtue of the war were out of work anyway. A number of these were commandeered by the Admiralty and fitted with the necessary equipment to deal with survivors, including a small operating theatre staffed by a naval surgeon and sick bay attendants. Scrambling nets were rigged on either side of the hull, and lifeboats were replaced by strong motor launches designed for rescue work. Officers and ratings were chosen for their expertise in seamanship and boat handling. Rescue ships were also fitted with high frequency direction finders (HF/DF) manned by naval personnel. Being at the rear of the convoy, bearings of U-boat radio transmissions taken by the rescue ship could produce a good cross with those of the escort leader, which was usually ahead of the convoy.

SC 107's allocated rescue ship was the ex-London & North Eastern Railway Company's *Stockport*. Completed in 1911, just nine months before the *Titanic* met her iceberg in the Atlantic, the 1,637-ton *Stockport* was a credit to her North-East Coast builders, in that after thirty gruelling years on the Harwich to the Hook of Holland cross-channel service she was still considered worthy of requisition by the Admiralty. She was first employed in July 1941 as a cable carrier for the Navy, and was converted as a rescue ship later in the year. Commanded by 39-year-old Captain Thomas Ernest Fea, she carried a crew of fifty-two merchant seamen. Also on board were Surgeon Lieutenant Neil Douglas, two sick bay attendants, eight gunners and one signaller, all seconded from the Royal Navy. Needless to say, those who manned the *Stockport* were a very special breed of men, not only experts in their various fields, but willing to put their own lives on the line to save others.

Also with SC 107 was the 2,153-ton ex-Lakes steamer USS *Gemini*. Built in the First World War, and requisitioned by the US Navy in August 1942 as a supply carrier, the *Gemini* was on her way to Iceland with a small number of military personnel on board.

Four days after sailing from New York, when abreast of Nova Scotia, SC 107 was joined by fourteen other ships from Halifax and Sydney, Cape Breton. The new arrivals were accompanied by two Canadian corvettes and a minesweeper. Various others came and went as the convoy made its way up the coast. Finally, on the afternoon of the

30 October, SC 107 was complete when five more ships joined from St John's, Newfoundland. The convoy then consisted of thirty-eight ships, and was a very cosmopolitan mix, being composed of eighteen British, six American, five Greek, four Norwegian, three Dutch, one Swedish and one Icelandic flag. With the latest arrivals came the convoy's ocean escort, consisting of the destroyer HMCS *Restigouche*, the corvettes *Algoma*, *Amherst* and *Arvida*, also of the RCN, and the British corvette *Celandine*. All other escorts then left.

Earlier in the month, the North Atlantic had been in an angry mood, with winds bordering on hurricane force and mountainous seas sweeping the open waters. This was not unusual on the approach of winter. One British shipmaster described the weather succinctly:

> We had three days of fog, followed by days of squalls of snow and rain. At times the cabins were knee-deep in sea-water. We ran before the gale – weather as thick as a hedge. I said, 'There'll be some fun if somebody heaves to and we don't see 'em', and soon after the ship ahead did: we saw her two red lights and went hard a-starboard and just missed her; had to go beam on to the sea to do it. This was about midnight, a thick, overcast night, black. The convoy was flattened out, partly dispersed, and we signalled some of the ships with Aldis to get 'em back. We hadn't quite reached the middle of the Atlantic then.

Now, conversely, the weather was almost benign, the wind light and variable, and apart from the interminable Atlantic swell, there was little movement in the sea. This was a welcome start to the voyage, but some of the old Western Ocean hands were already predicting fog. And well they might, for SC 107 was moving towards the Grand Banks of Newfoundland, where the warm waters of the Gulf Stream mingle with the cold Labrador Current generating ideal conditions for the formation of fog, dense and persistent.

Casting an experienced eye over the assembled convoy from the bridge of the *Jeypore*, leading ship of the centre column, Captain Tom Stevens approved of what he saw. He was less impressed with SC 107's meagre escort force.

Escort Group C-4, led by Lieutenant Commander Desmond Piers in *Restigouche*, was putting on a brave show of throwing a protective screen around the merchantmen, but even to the most inexperienced young galley boy emptying his gash bucket over the rails this was a pointless exercise. Piers just did not have enough ships.

In preparation for Operation Torch, 160 British destroyers and corvettes had been withdrawn from various theatres. This was achieved by temporarily suspending convoys to Russia and the South Atlantic, and by reducing escort forces in the North Atlantic. Needless to say, this was bound to have repercussions, one being that the defence of the trade convoys in the North Atlantic was almost entirely in the hands of the Royal Canadian Navy, a task for which it was ill prepared and ill equipped. At that time the Canadians had only seven destroyers, all elderly discards from the Royal Navy, and about sixty corvettes. Seventeen of the best of these corvettes had been commandeered for Torch, and of the remainder no more than twenty were available for convoy escort duty at any one time. The majority of the Canadian ships were less well equipped than their British counterparts, having only the near-obsolete Type SW radar, which was incapable of detecting U-boats on the surface except at very short range. Many were not fitted with gyro compass, and the men who crewed the ships, through no fault of their own, lacked training and experience in convoy work. Lieutenant James Barrett Lamb, RCNVR, who served in several Canadian corvettes, and commanded HMCS *Camrose*, wrote in later years:

> There was little enough to be proud of in the early days of the corvette navy. With experience and direction in such short supply, everything in a corvette depended upon the character and competence of the captain. If you were fortunate enough, as I was, to serve in a new ship commanded by an experienced merchant seaman, able to adapt to naval routines, you were one of a lucky minority; most of the new ships in the early months of the war were a shambles, and some were downright disgraceful. There was incompetence of every sort, at every level; some ships were barely able to get to sea, and once there, were fortunate to find their way back to port without mishap. Indiscipline was chronic, drunken captains, useless officers, mutinous crews were commonplace; those of us in the well-run ships grew to dread the prospect of new Canadian corvettes joining our group and tarnishing our Canadian image in the eyes of thunderstruck friends in British ships or bases. It was often all too easy to pick out the Canadian from a group of corvettes alongside; she was the dirty one with rusty sides, and with half her crew in tattered clothes of every sort, playing catch on the jetty.

It may seem that Lieutenant Lamb was being unduly harsh on his fellow Canadians, but he was there in the thick of the Battle of the Atlantic, and his comments must be regarded as credible.

There was also a scarcity of HF/DF sets in Canadian escorts. HF/DF, usually known as 'Huff Duff', was one of the most powerful Allied weapons in the fight against Dönitz's U-boats in the Second World War. The system was not new, the low and medium frequency radio direction finder having been used in navigation by ships world-wide since the 1920s. HF/DF, designed by the Royal Navy, used higher frequencies, producing reasonably accurate bearings on a U-boat using her radio out of visual and radar range. Given that German submarine commanders were notorious for radio chatter when shadowing a convoy, this was easily done. If two or more ships in the convoy were fitted with HF/DF it was possible to pinpoint with some accuracy the position of a U-boat. Errors crept in at greater distances, and for a U-boat transmitting in mid-Atlantic the fix might easily be 10–15 miles out. However, on occasions the result could be extremely accurate. To quote an example: on 29 June 1942, U-158, a long-range Type IXC under the command of Erwin Rostin, sank the Latvian-flag steamer *Everalda* when patrolling south of Bermuda. Confidential documents had been found on board the ship, and in conveying their contents to German U-boat headquarters at Lorient, Rostin indulged in a lengthy exchange of radio messages. Unknown to him, three US Navy direction finding stations were listening and taking bearings. Armed with the resulting fix, a Martin Mariner flying boat of US Navy Patrol Squadron 74 swooped on the surfaced U-boat, whose crew were caught sunbathing on deck. A well-aimed stick of depth charges went down, and U-158's patrol came to a swift and sudden end. She sank taking all fifty-four crew with her.

The Canadian ships were also disadvantaged by the acquisition by the U-boats in the early part of 1942 of the *Funkmessbeobachtung 1*, or to give it its more pronounceable name, *Metox*. Named after its French designer, Metox Grandin, this was a primitive, but effective, VHF radio receiver capable of detecting nearby radar transmissions. The receiver was situated in the U-boat's radio room and connected to a portable wooden aerial in the shape of a cross in the conning tower. Each time the submarine surfaced, the 'Biscay Cross', as the aerial became known, was taken up into the conning tower and mounted on its bracket where it could be rotated by hand. If radar transmissions were detected, an audible warning signal sounded, thereby, it was hoped, giving the U-boat time to dive before it was sighted visually. The one great weakness of *Metox* was that often, in the rush to clear the conning tower and get below the surface, the Biscay Cross was forgotten and subsequently lost during the crash dive. The tendency was not to bother taking the aerial aloft when surfacing.

The Canadian escort group C-4 had suffered a series of setbacks, beginning five weeks earlier while escorting a westbound convoy. ON 127 comprised thirty-two merchantmen, escorted by C-4, which was then at full strength and consisted of the destroyers *Ottawa* and *St Croix*, the corvettes *Amherst*, *Arvida* and *Sherbrooke*, with the British corvette *Celandine*. The convoy was attacked in the air gap in mid-ocean.

The *Black Pit*, known in official circles as the Air Gap, was a 'black hole' in North Atlantic air space between Greenland and Iceland which in 1942 was beyond the reach of most British and American based aircraft. At this stage of the war the few Very Long Range (VLR) planes capable of covering the Air Gap, largely four-engined Lockheed Liberator bombers, were fully occupied elsewhere, the RAF being committed to taking the war into the farthest reaches of Germany, while the US Air Force was heavily engaged with the Japanese in the Pacific. The Atlantic Air Gap was roughly 600 miles across, three and a half days steaming for the average convoy, during which time the ships were at their most vulnerable. It was here that the U-boat wolf packs laid their deadly ambushes, and here that the Allies were losing up to a hundred ships a month. It was a frightening haemorrhaging of ships and men which could not be long sustained.

As ON 127 was crossing the Air Gap it was set upon by a pack of twelve U-boats, and in a running fight lasting five days, seven of the merchant ships and the destroyer *Ottawa* were sunk. *Ottawa* went in the early hours of 12 September, when U-92 approached undetected and fired a spread of four torpedoes. Two of the torpedoes hit the *Ottawa* and left her unable to manoeuvre. She was easy meat when, two days later, Heinz Walkerling in U-91 found her and delivered the *coup de grâce*. Lieutenant Commander Rutherford, 115 of his men, and 16 survivors picked up earlier from the torpedoed tanker *Empire Oil* went down with the destroyer.

In addition to the ships sunk in ON 127, three other merchantmen were so badly damaged that they would be out of the war for a long time. Much of the blame for the heavy losses was put down to the C-4 escorts making excessive use of snowflake rockets. The U-boat commanders later commented that they were astonished at the apparent inexperience of the Canadian ships and that the indiscriminate use of snowflakes served no useful purpose, other than illuminating the convoy so that the ships were visible from miles around. The U-boats took full advantage of the helping hand they were unwittingly given, and earned themselves the honour of being the only attacking pack in which every U-boat fired all its torpedoes during the year. Only one of the U-boats received any damage in the attack, and that was superficial.

In addition to the loss of *Ottawa*, C-4 was also short of two corvettes, *Regina* and *Sherbrooke* having had to return to St John's for engine repairs. Of those that remained, only the British corvette *Celandine* had the new Type 271 radar, and the Asdic range of all the escorts, including *Restigouche*, was only 1,500 yards. The situation was not improved by two of the Canadian corvettes having had a change of command shortly before sailing. C-4 was a pitifully small, weak escort for such an important convoy, but due to the demands of Operation Torch it was the best available at the time, and as subsequent events would show, it was totally inadequate.

CHAPTER THREE

A Bunch of Violets

On 19 October, five days before SC107 sailed from New York, the Convoy & Routing Section of the C-in-C US Fleet (COMINCH) had radioed full details of the convoy and its projected route to all Allied commands concerned. As German Naval Intelligence was at the time routinely decrypting all such messages, this proved to be an open invitation to Dönitz and his U-boats to intervene, and Lorient immediately set about preparing a reception committee. All boats patrolling in the area were called in, and Group *Veilchen* (Violet) was formed. When complete, *Veilchen* consisted of thirteen Type VII boats, namely U-71, U-84, U-89, U-132, U-381, U-402, U-437, U-438, U-442, U-454, U-571, U-658 and U-704. A 150-mile-long patrol line was then set up some 400 miles to the north-east of Newfoundland, stretching in a north-west/south-east direction across SC107's track. Additionally, Dönitz recalled the three Type IX long-range boats U-520, U-521 and U-522, then heading west near St John's. And it was one of this trio, U-522, that first confirmed the existence of Convoy SC107.

U-522, under the command of 27-year-old Kapitänleutnant Herbert Schneider, was on her first operational patrol, and had left Kiel only three weeks earlier. Her original briefing had called for her, along with U-520 and U-521, to take up station in the approaches to the Gulf of St Lawrence.

It was only by a quirk of fate that Admiral Dönitz discovered that the Gulf of St Lawrence offered another 'happy hunting ground' for his U-boats.

In the early summer of 1942, U-553, under the command of Karl Thurmann, was operating off the American Eastern Seaboard against convoys from New York to Halifax and Sydney, Nova Scotia, when she began to experience engine troubles. Thurmann decided to take refuge in the calmer waters of the Gulf of St Lawrence, where he hoped to be able to carry out repairs undisturbed.

The Gulf of St Lawrence, a vast deep-water estuary 430 miles long by 80 miles wide, had up until then been free of U-boats, and ships loading in the Gulf ports were sailing unescorted to the convoy assembly ports in Nova Scotia. The Royal Canadian Navy, then bearing the brunt of escort duty for the transatlantic convoys, had reduced its force in the Gulf to one Bangor-class minesweeper, two Fairmile Marine motor launches, and an armed yacht. With such a wide area to cover, it follows that merchant ships within the Gulf were given little or no protection.

On the morning of 12 May, the British steamer *Nicoya* was passing south of Anticosti Island on passage from Montreal to Avonmouth via Halifax. Owned by Elders & Fyffes of London, the 5,346-ton *Nicoya* was under the command of Captain Ernest Brice, and had on board a total complement of eighty-eight, including ten passengers. In times of peace, her distinctive white hull and upperworks were a familiar sight in the Caribbean, as she moved from island to island picking up bananas for Liverpool. Now, in her new wartime role, she carried a cargo of frozen beef, steel and glass, with Hurricane fighter aircraft on her hatch-tops. It was the *Nicoya*'s deck cargo that caught Karl Thurmann's eye.

Thurmann had been stalking the *Nicoya* since before midnight on the 11th, and by dawn on the 12th was at periscope depth ahead of the unsuspecting ship. U-553 was within 450 yards of the *Nicoya* when Thurmann fired his first torpedo, hitting her in her after cargo hold. Adjacent to this hold was the magazine for the 4-inch gun, containing in the region of 700lbs of high explosive. Fortunately, much of the blast of the resulting explosion was absorbed by the beef in the hold, but the ship was crippled, her propeller and rudder smashed, her hull breached. Thurmann finished her off with a second torpedo twenty minutes later.

Six men died in the blast, but Captain Brice and the remainder of his crew and passengers took to the boats, and reached the safety of the nearby shore. They were unaware that they had made history. The *Nicoya* was the first ship ever to be sunk by enemy action in Canadian waters, and the six men who lost their lives were the first to die in the Gulf from enemy fire since the Anglo-American war of 1812.

Before leaving the Gulf of St Lawrence, U-553 also sank the 4,712-ton Dutch steamer *Leto*. Karl Thurmann's brief sortie into the Gulf caused severe political repercussions in Canada, resulting in some escorts being withdrawn from the Atlantic, and thereafter merchant ships sailed in convoy in the Gulf.

Shortly after noon on 29 October, U-522 was 50 miles to the southeast of Cape Race, and on her way to the Gulf of St Lawrence, when she sighted the masts and funnels of SC 107. Schneider radioed news of the sighting to Lorient, and was instructed to shadow the convoy at a safe distance, reporting every two hours. Meanwhile U-520 and U-521 were ordered to join Schneider at all possible speed.

As might be expected, the assembling of the thirteen boats of *Veilchen* and the recall of the Type IXs had involved a great deal of radio traffic between Lorient and the U-boats, and between the boats themselves. Although the signals were coded and sent at ultra-high speeds, they were sufficient for DF stations in Newfoundland to establish with some accuracy the whereabouts of the wolf pack. The destroyer HMCS *Columbia*, under the command of Lieutenant Commander G.H. Stephen DSC, RCNR, then on her way back to St John's, was ordered to rejoin SC 107, and reconnaissance aircraft were scrambled to begin a search.

At 1205 on the 30th, *Columbia* sighted an unidentified object on the horizon at about 7 miles. She immediately altered course to investigate. A few minutes later, the target was seen to be a U-boat on the surface. Stephen increased speed to 23 knots and sent his men to action stations.

Either Herbert Schneider had been complacent, or his lookouts had not been alert enough, but U-522 suddenly found herself to be the quarry of a very determined Canadian destroyer. At first believing his pursuer to be a 16-knot corvette armed with a single 4-inch gun, Schneider tried to run away on the surface, but soon found he was being overtaken. When salvoes of 4.7-inch shells began to bracket the U-boat, Schneider decided it was time to take cover below the surface. What followed was the classic cat and mouse routine, with U-522 caught in *Columbia's* Asdic beam and twisting and turning to avoid the shower of depth charges raining down on her. Schneider attempted to counter attack by firing a spread of two torpedoes, but the destroyer easily avoided them. The chase continued into the night until, at 2000, *Columbia* lost all contact. U-522 lived to fight another day.

U-658, commanded by Kapitänleutnant Hans Senkel, and also on her first war patrol, was stationed at the far south-eastern end of the *Veilchen* line, with little prospect of playing a major part in the coming convoy battle. This was Senkel's second patrol in command of U-658. His first voyage had yielded the very satisfying score of three ships totalling 12,146 tons sunk, and another 6,000-tonner damaged. He was now anxious to add to that score and on the morning of the 30th he decided to move closer to the action. By mid-afternoon, he was directly in the path of SC 107, and made the mistake of surfacing to take a better look around the horizon.

The two Lockheed Hudsons of 145 Squadron RCAF were on an anti-submarine sweep from their base in Newfoundland, and were nearing the limit of their endurance when U-658's conning tower broke the surface. Flying Officer Edward La Page Robinson, piloting the lead Hudson, immediately dived to attack, bracketing the surfacing U-boat with four 250lb depth charges, all of which fell within 15 feet of U-658. She was blown out of the water before Senkel had chance to open the conning tower hatch. Her pressure hull was blown wide open, and with all her buoyancy gone she slid under, leaving only a patch of disturbed water and a spreading oil slick to mark her grave. Hans Senkel and his crew of forty-seven went to join the list of dead recorded on the U-boat memorial at Möltenort, near Kiel.

Later that day, a Douglas Digby, piloted by Flying Officer Daniel Raymes, was returning to its base at Gander after covering an inbound convoy, when another U-boat was sighted on the surface. This was U-520, one of the trio of long-range boats originally bound for the Gulf of St Lawrence. Commanded by Volkmar Schwartzkopff, she had sailed from Kiel nearly a month earlier, and was 50 miles off the east coast of Newfoundland when she received orders to join Group *Veilchen*. Being then on her maiden war patrol with no Allied ships to her credit, it seems likely that in his haste to join the action Schwartz-kopff had thrown caution to the winds, and stayed on the surface longer than it was safe to do so. On sighting the surfaced submarine, FO Raymes went straight in to attack, banking sharply to port and coming up astern of U-520 just as she was disappearing below the surface. The Digby's four 450lb depth charges followed her down, and exploded around her as one. U-520's bow reared up out of the mael-strom created by the exploding charges, then slid under again, leaving a dark slick of oil spreading on the water. Volkmar Schwartskopff and his crew of fifty-two went down with their as yet unblooded boat. It had been a good day for the Royal Canadian Air Force, a bad day for Dönitz's U-boats.

Steaming in nine columns abreast, with the Group C-4 escorts making a brave attempt to guard the perimeter, Convoy SC 107 may have been an impressive sight to the casual observer, but a closer look would have revealed how vulnerable the merchant ships were. By and large, they were no-nonsense Western Ocean tramps, most of them of a certain age, all rust-stained and sagging under the weight of heavy cargoes. The oldest of the flock, the 3,189-ton Greek-flag *Parthenon*, had first tasted salt water in 1908 when the last of the great windjammers were still challenging Cape Horn. Another Greek, the *Agios Georgios*, dated from 1911, while the British-flag *Maritima*'s maiden voyage had coincided with that of the ill-fated *Titanic*. Only a year younger, the 4,474-ton *Oropos*, with her tall natural-draft funnel and counter stern, was so low in the water with her cargo of grain that she appeared to be sinking. Several others were of First World War vintage, and there was not one amongst them able to sustain much more than 9 knots. In deference to their collective antiquity and defects, wise heads at the Admiralty had set the convoy speed at 7½ knots, which is the pace of an unhurried cyclist, a speed that any U-boat then prowling the North Atlantic could match underwater. And of these, growing numbers appeared to be in the vicinity of the convoy. Captain Arthur Hawkins, commanding the 7,459-ton *Empire Sunrise*, rear ship of the starboard outside column, later wrote: 'I was receiving messages of submarine sightings long before we got clear of Newfoundland. When these were placed on the chart it was plain to see we were heading into a pack of U-boats.'

The London-registered *Empire Sunrise*, owned by Lawther, Latta & Company and built in Sunderland in 1941, was on her way from Three Rivers, on the St Lawrence River, to Belfast with 10,000 tons of steel and timber, much of the timber being carried as deck cargo. She was manned by a British crew of fifty-one, which included five DEMS gunners.

The practice of arming British merchant ships goes back to the eighteenth century, when piracy was rife on the high seas, and the slow, heavily-laden merchantmen were at the mercy of a host of armed enemies. Many of the ships of the Honorable East India Company, carrying high value cargoes home from the East, were as well armed as the men-of-war of the Royal Navy.

When the cumbersome, square-rigged East Indiamen gave way to the fast clipper ships, guns became largely irrelevant, until the First World War threatened. When it became apparent that Germany would blockade British waters, Winston Churchill, then First Lord of the Admiralty, despite opposition from his peers, reintroduced heavy arms aboard merchant ships, specifying, as per the Geneva Convention, that they should be for defence only. In reality, this meant a single 4-inch on the stern, to be used when being pursued by a submarine. The net result of this was the dumping of the gentlemanly Prize Rules by the German Navy, and unrestricted submarine warfare. However, thanks to Churchill, British merchant seamen had the chance to hit back at their enemies.

On the outbreak of war again in September 1939, the anti-submarine guns mothballed in 1918 were dusted off and brought back into service. By the end of the year, nearly 50 per cent of ocean-going ships were defensively armed. At first, ships' crews, many of whom had never handled anything more lethal than a marlin spike, manned the guns, but after the fall of France in 1940 trained gunners of the Royal Navy and Maritime Anti-Aircraft Regiment Royal Artillery were put aboard the ships. The Defensively Equipped Merchant Ship (DEMS) gunners, usually six to ten per ship, manned and maintained all guns, assisted when required by crew members, many of whom had been given a short course in gunnery. The system worked well, although there were few opportunities to engage the U-boats, who either attacked after dark on the surface, or from periscope depth during the day.

Captain Hawkins was correct in his observations. SC 107 had been first sighted by U-522 when the rendezvous was made with the feeder convoys off St John's on the 29th. She had been chased away by HMCS *Columbia*, but regained contact later in the afternoon. Schneider resumed sending two-hourly reports to Lorient, while at the same time acting as a homing beacon for the other *Veilchen* boats. Once again the ether was alive with radio transmissions, and the HF/DF operators aboard *Restigouche* and SC 107's rescue ship *Stockport* were kept busy logging a continuous stream of bearings.

During the morning of 1 November some twenty-five HF/DF fixes were obtained, indicating that at least eight U-boats were following in the wake of the convoy. SC 107 was by then on the extreme limit of air cover from Newfoundland and about to enter the notorious 'Black Pit', where the U-boats were free to hunt unmolested. Lieutenant Commander Piers requested air cover, and a Canso flying boat of 116 Squadron RCAF was sent out, more as a parting gesture than anything else. However, the Canso did surprise a U-boat on the surface 9 miles astern of the convoy and reported the sighting to *Restigouche*.

The shadowing U-boat was Wilhelm-Heinrich Graf Pückler und Limpurg's U-381, a Type VIIC on her first Atlantic war patrol. She had been following the convoy for some time, and when spotted from the air she was engaged in radioing to Lorient the convoy's position, course and speed. Her transmissions enabled *Restigouche* and *Stockport* to obtain an HF/DF fix. *Restigouche* increased to 20 knots and ran down the line of bearing. At the same time, Piers signalled the convoy commodore to make an emergency turn to port in an attempt to shake off the shadower. Minutes later, *Restigouche*'s radar showed a small blip ahead, and the conning tower of a U-boat was sighted.

U-381 dived as soon as the avenging destroyer was seen bearing down on her. Lieutenant Commander Piers reduced speed and began an Asdic search, picking up the submerged U-boat without difficulty. Running over the spot, he attacked with depth charges, but he was too late. U-381 had gone deep and was creeping away.

By mid-afternoon, Piers had a clear idea of what the coming night would bring, and he found himself praying for the arrival of the dense fog so often prevalent in the area, despite the fearful danger of multiple collisions within the convoy it might bring.

Perversely, the Grand Banks of Newfoundland did not live up to their age old reputation. The weather remained fair, with the North Atlantic showing an unusually kindly face. The wind, no more than a light breeze, was in the north-west and the sea relatively quiet, except for the long undulating swell. The overcast sky was beginning to break up and visibility was good. Piers welcomed the coming of darkness like an old and trusty friend, but when the sun went down it was replaced by the flickering light of the Aurora Borealis which showed up the ships in sharp relief. For the gathering U-boats of Group *Veilchen* even nature seemed to be on their side. The weather conditions for an attack could not have been better.

The HF/DF bearings were still coming in, and Piers sent HMS *Celandine* to investigate the nearest of these transmissions, which appeared to originate about 8 miles astern on the port quarter of the convoy. *Restigouche* then made a sweep further astern in search of other U-boats, but failed to find any.

Unlike *Celandine*, which had the modern 271M radar, *Restigouche* carried a SW1C set, the Canadian version of the outdated British 286PQ radar. This had been designed as an aircraft radar, with maximum range of 7 miles in favourable weather conditions. It was a primitive set with an aerial at the masthead rotated by a hand-cranked mechanism, echoes showing up on a cathode ray tube as peaks, much the same as on a heart monitor, giving approximate range and bearing.

At 1904, *Restigouche* was 6 miles astern of the convoy when her radar operator reported an echo bearing 325 degrees at 1,800 yards. Piers rang for 20 knots and moved in to investigate. Starshell fired revealed a U-boat on the surface. *Restigouche* gave chase, but the U-boat dived. Minutes later a strong Asdic contact was picked up at 300 yards on the destroyer's starboard bow. Piers ran over the spot, dropping a pattern of depth charges, the explosion of which knocked one of *Restigouche*'s dynamos off the board causing a failure of the destroyer's steering. The U-boat escaped.

The thump of the depth charges and the bursting starshell caused a minor panic amongst some of the more nervous merchantmen, who added to the display by firing their snowflake rockets. The net result of the starshell, the snowflakes and the aurora borealis was to turn night into day, further increasing the vulnerability of the already exposed ships.

With *Restigouche* and *Celandine* both away, the defence of the convoy was left to the three Canadian corvettes *Algoma*, *Arvida* and *Amherst*. *Arvida*, commanded by Temporary Lieutenant Dudley King, RCNVR, was guarding the starboard side of the convoy, and at this crucial moment her radar set had broken down. The waiting enemy was quick to take advantage.

U-402, a Type VIIC launched at Danzig in the winter of 1940, had sailed out of La Pallice on the night of 4 October with orders to join Group *Panther*, which was then setting up a patrol line across the main convoy route in mid-Atlantic. She was on her fifth war patrol under the command of Kapitänleutnant Siegfried Freiherr von Forstner.

Siegfried von Forstner, born in Hanover in 1910, had entered the German Navy as an officer cadet in April 1930. He saw service in the pocket-battleships *Admiral Scheer* and *Deutschland*, and when war came again in 1939, he was in the light cruiser *Nürnberg*. He transferred to the U-boat arm in April 1940, and served one patrol with the fabled Otto Kretschmer in U-99 before taking command of U-402. Born into an aristocratic Prussian family, Forstner had a formidable tradition to live up to. His great-grandfather and grandfather had both been distinguished Army officers, an uncle had commanded U-boats in the 1914-18 war, and his father, General Ernst Freiherr von Forstner, had been awarded the coveted Blue Max in the same conflict. Of Siegfried's generation, his younger brother was also a U-boat commander, and two other brothers were Army officers.

U-402 joined the other boats of *Panther* on 12 October, the intention being to ambush and attack the westbound convoy ONS 136. After a frustrating week spent searching empty horizons, the North Atlantic weather decided to take a hand. An entry in Dönitz's War Diary for 19 October reads:

Operation on ON-convoy turned out to be a total failure on account of bad weather. The fog which gathered three hours after the first sighting led to a loss of contact and bad damage to U-609 which was engaged on submerged attack when the fog came down.

Continuous fog and heavy westerly storm with wind up to strength 11 made organized search impossible and hindered a successful operation on the part of twenty-five boats ...

Despite the hostile weather, ONS 136 was intercepted and Group *Panther* was joined by two other packs, *Leopard* and *Wotan*, in a combined attack on the convoy. In poor visibility and high seas, four Allied merchantmen were sunk. In retaliation, U-609 was heavily depth charged and so badly damaged that she was forced to return to Lorient. Group *Panther* was later disbanded and U-402 was sent west to join the assembling Group *Veilchen*, which by then was closing in on Convoy SC 107 further to the west.

At around noon on Sunday, 1 November, von Forstner received a sighting report from U-381, which was then in visual contact with Convoy SC 107. Anxious to close with the enemy at last, von Forstner increased to full speed and set course for the position given, which was about 30 miles to the north-east. An hour later, with von Forstner in the conning tower, U-402 was breasting the waves at an unprecedented 18 knots when she was almost caught off-guard. A warning shout from the after lookout brought von Forstner spinning round just in time to see a Canso flying boat dropping out of the clouds astern. He slammed the klaxon and cleared the conning tower in seconds, but U-402 was still only half-submerged when the aircraft roared overhead. By the grace of God, or whatever other being was watching over Siegfried von Forstner and his men on that day, the Canso's depth charges failed to drop. The Canadian flying boat must have been operating at the very extreme edge of its range, for when U-402 surfaced again an hour later the aircraft was nowhere to be seen.

Darkness had long fallen by the time U-402 reached the position given by U-381's report. The moon was not yet up, but visibility was good, and by 2000 von Forstner had dark shadows on the horizon ahead that grew into the silhouettes of eastbound ships as U-402 moved closer. She was approaching the outer starboard column of

Convoy SC 107. At 2058 von Forstner fired a single torpedo aimed at the rear ship of the column. The torpedo failed to leave its tube. Five minutes later he fired again, this time with more success.

Lieutenant John M. Waters, US Coastguard, aboard the supply ship USS *Gemini*, witnessed the result:

First came the dull shock as a torpedo hit *Empire Sunrise* 3 miles away, then the shrill clanging of the *Gemini*'s general alarm bell. In the compartment, illuminated only by a dim red light, men piled out of their bunks, attempting simultaneously to don clothing and life jackets. On the main deck they were greeted by an unforgettable sight. Every ship in the convoy was firing snowflakes, lighting the scene like daylight, and as they burned the noise of depth charges was heard again.

As the months passed, this feeling would become engraved in the minds of many as one of the prime ingredients of a night combat action at sea. The usual reaction to the crash of a torpedo is fright, a sudden natural animal fright, accompanied by the pounding pulse, cold sweat and, as time goes on, by paradoxical yawns. Men forced to wait under extreme stress often tend to yawn, and on the deck of the *Gemini*, bathed in a flickering light from the snowflakes and the burning *Dalcroy*, the yawning spread contagiously.

We new ensigns, together with several more senior officers and 200 army troops, were loaded aboard the USS *Gemini*, an antiquated freighter, for transport overseas to join our ship.

Due to a negligence by the ship's officers, nearly half of *Gemini*'s passengers had no life jackets. After the attacks started, the ship's two 3-inch guns were manned continuously, and the passenger officers stood watches as battery officers with the ship's gun crews. En route to relieve a gun watch, I worked my way along the deck in the darkness toward the aft 3-incher. The night was cold and flurries of snow rode the heavy wind gusts. If we were hit, which seemed a distinct possibility, there would be little chance for survival, and none without a life jacket. Then my hand came in contact with a circular object – a life ring mounted on the rail. Cutting it loose, I slung the life ring over my shoulder and continued aft to relieve the battery officer. The gun captain, a regular Navy bosun's mate who had survived the sinking of the carrier USS *Lexington* several months before, looked at me in my steel helmet with the life ring draped over my shoulder. Laughing, he said, 'I'll tell you one thing, sir, they ain't never gonna use a picture of you in a recruiting poster!'

Captain Arthur Hawkins of the *Empire Sunrise*, sailing as fourth ship of SC 107's Column 9, takes up the story:

We proceeded without incident until 1915 on 1 November when star shells were fired astern of us. I also heard depth charges being released at the same time. At 2100 I heard the sound of a motor engine just forward of our starboard beam and at 2105 the conning tower of a submarine was seen just forward of our starboard beam. I immediately put the helm hard to starboard with the intention of ramming the submarine which was following a parallel course. The submarine appeared to turn towards my ship and almost at the same time I noticed a thin streak coming in our direction. I realised that a torpedo had been fired, so ran to the centre of the bridge and shouted to everyone in the vicinity to take cover. At 2107 on 1 November when in position 51.50 N 46.25 W a torpedo struck the ship abreast of No. 2 hold on the starboard side. There was a heavy swell at the time with light airs, the weather was fine and the visibility good. We were proceeding at a speed of 7½ knots on a course of 010 degrees.

When the *Empire Sunrise* was torpedoed, HMCS *Restigouche* was 6 miles astern of the convoy hunting a U-boat that had been sighted on the surface. This would account for Captain Hawkins' report of seeing starshell and hearing depth charges exploding. *Restigouche* had in fact dropped a pattern of ten charges on another unidentified U-boat that had penetrated the convoy. It was subsequently learned that U-381's sighting report had brought in five other U-boats apart from U-402, all of which appeared to have penetrated the defensive screen. This is perhaps not surprising, as when U-402 made the first strike against SC 107, not only was *Restigouche* away, but the British corvette *Celandine*, the only escort with an effective radar set, was 8 miles off on the port quarter investigating a HF/DF fix, and at that crucial moment her radar had broken down. The immediate defence of the convoy was in the hands of the three Canadian corvettes *Algoma*, *Amherst* and *Arvida*, none of which possessed HF/DF or a modern radar.

On receiving word from the rescue ship *Stockport* that the *Empire Sunrise* had been torpedoed, Lieutenant Commander Piers in

Restigouche ordered all escorts to carry out Operation Raspberry. This involved each ship turning outwards and firing starshell, the object being to illuminate any U-boats that might be on the surface. The wisdom of this manoeuvre has often been questioned, as it was on this occasion by Captain Hawkins of the *Empire Sunrise*. He later wrote:

> I would like to protest against the continued firing of snowflakes by ships of this convoy which I think gave the convoy away. If, when attacked on the starboard side by a submarine, snowflakes are released, the whole of that side of the convoy is illuminated for a submarine which may be lurking on the port side waiting to attack.

Captain Hawkins may not have articulated the case against the use of starshell, or snowflakes, very well, but as an experienced convoy man he was acutely aware of the danger of lighting up the scene, so that all the ships of the convoy, before just dark smudges on the horizon, were shown up in stark silhouette. As it turned out, Lieutenant Commander Piers' Operation Raspberry did just that, and nothing more. No U-boats were sighted.

Although the *Empire Sunrise* was obviously hard hit by Siegfried von Forstner's torpedo, she showed no immediate signs of sinking. Captain Hawkins explained in his report to the Admiralty:

> The ship remained on an even keel. I stopped the engines immediately after the explosion, fired two of our white rockets and told the Wireless Operator to send out a wireless signal. This he was unable to do as the foremast had crashed, bringing down the main wireless aerial which fell on the emergency aerial and shorted it. This was soon cleared and at 2120 a message was sent out on the auxiliary set, which was acknowledged by the Commodore.
>
> I also sounded six blasts on our steam whistle and mustered the crew on deck, but gave strict orders that nothing was to be touched on the boat deck as the ship was in no immediate danger of sinking. At 2123 the ship still remained upright and I thought we had a good chance of proceeding, so I ordered the engineers and firemen below, and at 2130 full speed was rung on the engine room telegraph, with the intention of rejoining the convoy.
>
> At 2145 the rescue ship *Stockport* came up on our starboard side and signaled 'Are you all right?' I replied that my compasses were not working but that I was trying to keep going to catch up with

the convoy. The *Stockport* replied that she would stand by and assist me with my course. At 2245 I sent the 3rd Officer down to the main deck to get some idea of our freeboard at that time. He returned and told me that we had no more than 4 feet freeboard which meant we had settled 8 feet by the head in two hours.

At 2300 there was a violent rending and grating noise just forward of the bridge on the port side which sounded to me very much as if the rivets were breaking. I immediately stopped the ship and sounded the alarm as I thought the ship was breaking in two. The noise continued, so I decided to abandon ship.

With some difficulty, caused by the heavy swell, Hawkins and his men abandoned the *Empire Sunrise* in two lifeboats, and were picked up by the *Stockport*, which had continued to stand by the stricken ship. While the rescue was in progress, *Restigouche* joined them and used her searchlight to examine the *Empire Sunrise*. The powerful light revealed a gaping hole, described by Captain Hawkins as '10 feet by 9 feet' in the ship's waterline forward of her bridge. Any thought of salvaging her was out of the question. Nevertheless, when he and his men were safely aboard the rescue ship, Hawkins sent a message to the Commodore requesting that he be allowed to reboard his ship at daylight, if she was still afloat. His request was refused on the grounds that no escort could be spared to stand by the *Empire Sunrise*. When Captain Hawkins last saw his ship just after midnight, her main deck was awash and she was so far down by the head that her propeller was partly out of the water. Hawkins estimated that she had no more than six hours to live. In fact, an hour and ten minutes later the abandoned ship was sighted by Horst Uphoff in U-84, and he promptly dispatched her and her cargo to the bottom.

CHAPTER FOUR

Ambushed

From the moment that Siegfried von Forstner's torpedo homed in on the *Empire Sunrise* the much-depleted Escort Group C-4 had been in a state of some disarray. More than half an hour elapsed before the destroyer *Restigouche*, which had been chasing shadows astern of the convoy, came racing back to deal with the attacking U-boat. She arrived on the scene in time to see U-402's conning tower disappearing below the surface. Canadian Navy chaplain J.M. Armstrong, who was aboard the *Restigouche* at his own request to experience convoy warfare at first hand, later recorded his impressions:

> We had scarcely settled down from this first attack when at 0315Z on 2 November the general action station bell went again. Men do not take long in the Navy to answer that bell. To the hum of the engines was added the further sound of men rushing hither and yon to their particular action stations. These men did not walk, not even walk fast – they ran. I found myself running too, but not as rapidly as the others, for the ship was new to me, and I collided with rigging or stumbled over an eye bolt on the deck in the pitch dark. I was not going up the ladder to the fo'c'sle fast enough for those behind me. They told me to 'get cracking'. I did ... We found that the bell had not been rung for practice by any means. The convoy had been attacked.

U-402 went deep to avoid *Restigouche*'s depth charges and crept away, shaken but undamaged. It was near midnight before von Forstner deemed it safe to re-emerge from the depths, and when he did U-402 was on the port side of the convoy. By this time it seemed that every ship in the convoy was firing snowflakes, and the dark night had been turned into day. In the flickering light of the bursting rockets von Forstner could clearly see the ships of the port outer column in sharp relief. Leading was the 4,640-ton West Hartlepool tramp *Daleby*, staggering under an 8,500-ton cargo of bulk grain, topped off with tanks on deck. Following her was another North-East coaster, the

4,558-ton *Dalcroy* owned by Campbell Brothers of Newcastle-upon-Tyne and carrying 1,809 tons of steel and 6,000 tons of timber from St John, New Brunswick to the Tyne. She was very deep in the water, with timber piled 12 feet high on her decks. Next in line was the Greek-owned *Rinos*, loaded with general for Hull, and bringing up the rear was another Greek-flag, the 4,474-ton *Oropos*, of 1913-vintage, and also carrying grain.

The choice of targets presented to Siegfried von Forstner required little selection. All four ships were deep-loaded and ambling along at a snail's pace. The leading ship, *Daleby*, down to her marks and with tanks on deck, was the obvious priority, and von Forstner took aim at her and fired a single torpedo. It was a miss, the torpedo skimming across past the stern of the *Daleby* to detonate on the other side of her. Von Forstner chose another target and fired again.

Captain John Johnson, commanding the *Dalcroy*, had been on the bridge since early evening on the 1st when *Restigouche* had her first brush with the U-boats. Later, when the *Empire Sunrise*, on the far side of the convoy, had been torpedoed he had manned all his guns and sent his crew to their action stations. There had been little sleep for anyone in the *Dalcroy* on that long night. Now, in the small hours of the 2nd, Johnson was tired, as were all those on the bridge with him. The convoy reached a position 350 miles due east of Belle Isle, and the *Dalcroy* was rolling lazily in the long westerly swell. It was a quiet night, the sky heavily overcast, the darkness complete, and despite their state of alert no one saw von Forstner's second torpedo streaking towards them.

The torpedo struck at 0015, hitting the *Dalcroy* in her No. 2 hold, just forward of the bridge. Captain Johnson described events in his report to the Admiralty:

> The explosion was not very loud when the torpedo struck my ship and the ship only vibrated slightly. I did not see any flame, nor was the track of the torpedo seen as it approached the ship ... Immediately the torpedo struck I went to switch on the red lights and fire the rockets but everything had disappeared from the bridge and as the chart room was completely wrecked I could not get into it to get further supplies. The port boat had disappeared, my room and all midship accommodation was wrecked, and the port wing of the bridge seemed to have disappeared. The plastic protection on the port side of the bridge had also collapsed. We

had an oil red lamp in case the electric light failed but this was blown across the wheel house and smashed.

A wireless message was sent out, but I do not know if this was received; No. 11 ahead of us also sent out a wireless signal stating that we had been torpedoed.

The magnetic compasses were destroyed but the Browns gyro compass continued working perfectly and the steering gear remained in order. As a large portion of our cargo was timber I thought the ship might remain afloat so I continued with the convoy. Half an hour later the ship took a very heavy list to port, the Chief Engineer reported that he was unable to close the water-tight doors into the bunker hold, and that the engine room and stoke hold were rapidly filling with water.

Over the course of the next hour the *Dalcroy*'s list increased steadily until the ship was lying over at an angle of 45–50 degrees. She was virtually on her beam ends, shipping water over her port bulwarks at every roll. Standing upright was a near impossibility, and a quiet air of inevitability lay over the ship. People were uneasy, but no one panicked.

Finally, at 0100, when it was clear that the *Dalcroy* would not last much longer, Johnson gave the order to take to the boats. He wrote in his report:

I saw the starboard boat away first as it was on the high side, after which I got into the port boat, being able to step off the deck into it.

I never thought for a minute of abandoning the ship, but thought it was wise to get the crew clear of the ship and then at daylight to reboard if she was still afloat ...

Morning never came for the *Dalcroy*. When the sun rose on 2 November, she was gone. Later, Captain Johnson and his crew, all uninjured and in good spirits, were picked up by the rescue ship *Stockport*.

Restigouche was on the convoy's starboard quarter when U-402 began her attack and Lieutenant Commander Piers immediately hauled the destroyer around and crossed astern of the merchant ships at full speed. Within minutes the Asdic operator reported a 'sub' contact at 900 yards, and Piers moved in to attack, firing a ten-charge pattern of depth charges. The only apparent result of the subsequent explosion was as before, one of *Restigouche*'s dynamos being blown off the board, with a temporary loss of steering. When back in control, Piers tried another ten-charge attack, but it was too late. The bird had flown. But before leaving von Forstner had fired a parting salvo of two torpedoes.

Immediately astern of the *Dalcroy* in Column 1 was the Greek steamer *Rinos*, a no-nonsense, box-like tramp of 4,649 tons built in Sunderland in 1919. Launched as the *Westcliff* for the obscure Cliffside Shipping Company of Newcastle, she was sold to Swedish owners a year later, and in 1936 ended up under the house flag of Leonidas Embiricos, one of the numerous Greek shipowners with offices in Piraeus. Now, at the mature age of 23 years, with her ageing three-cylinder engine hard pressed to maintain the convoy speed of 7½ knots, the *Rinos* was an easy target for one of Siegfried von Forstner's torpedoes.

With her rust-weakened bottom plates blown open, the *Rinos*, weighed down by 6,000 tons of general cargo, began to sink at once. Captain Dimitrios Lekkas ordered the lifeboats to be lowered, but as they went down the *Rinos* capsized, and most of her crew of thirty-one ended up in the water.

The corvette *Amherst*, commanded by Lieutenant Commander Louis de la Chesnaye Audette, RCNVR, was guarding the port wing of the convoy when U-402 struck. She obtained a positive Asdic contact at 1,500 yards and raced in to attack with depth charges.

Approaching the target area, Audette became aware of a cluster of tiny red lights bobbing on the water directly over the spot he intended to drop his charges. These, he realized with horror, were the lifejacket lights of survivors in the water.

Audette was faced with a nightmare decision: if he went ahead and dropped his depth charges, it would be certain death for those men in the water, and if he held back, the U-boat beneath them would surely get away. Some years later, Audette said, 'I couldn't leave the submarine. I held him on Asdic. I couldn't leave him free to kill more men, sink more ships and their cargoes – and there were hundreds of other men in the convoy still.' Mercifully, Audette was spared the need to make that life-or-death decision. As he approached the survivors, *Amherst*'s Asdic failed, and Audette was obliged to call off the attack.

As *Amherst* withdrew, the rescue ship *Stockport* moved in to take her place. For Captain Thomas Fea and his men the night had only just begun. They already had on board fifty-one survivors from the *Empire Sunrise* and forty-nine from the *Dalcroy*, all taken from their boats, but now there were men in the water who needed their help, and they must be picked up quickly, or they would die in the icy Atlantic.

As Captain Fea manoeuvred the *Stockport* nearer the survivors, a dark shape suddenly loomed up ahead. It was the *Rinos*, floating bottom-up and positioned to add disaster to an already troubled night if the *Stockport* collided with her. Only quick thinking and brilliant ship handling by Fea saved the *Stockport*.

More fine seamanship by the *Stockport*'s chief officer, 33-year-old Herbert Earnshaw, saved the lives of the men in the water. Making use of one of the Greek ship's damaged and waterlogged lifeboats, Earnshaw and a volunteer crew snatched twenty-six of the *Rinos*' crew of thirty-one from the water, and battled back to the *Stockport* against a rising sea. Chief Officer Earnshaw was so exhausted when he reached the rescue ship's side, that he lost his grip on the scrambling net as he was boarding and fell back into the sea. Only prompt action by his crew saved him from certain death.

The second strike against SC 107 by the *Veilchen* boats was two-pronged. While U-402 was engaged in sinking ships in the outer port column, U-522 was making a stealthy approach from the south.

U-522, a Type IXC long-range boat under the command of Kapitän-leutnant Herbert Schneider, was on her first war patrol, and had yet to sink an enemy ship. Commissioned in Hamburg in June 1942 by Schneider, a 27-year-old ex-Luftwaffe officer who had seen service in the Spanish Civil War, U-522 had sailed from Kiel on 8 October. Schneider's orders were to take up station off Newfoundland after first reconnoitring the sea around Greenland's Cape Farewell, through which Allied convoys were said to be passing.

Escorted by patrol boats, U-522 followed the coast of Norway until in latitude 62° North, then altered westwards to pass between the Shetland Islands and the Faroes, reaching the open Atlantic four days later. She arrived in the vicinity of Cape Farewell on 15 October, but after forty-eight hours without encountering a single ship, decided to move on south. Off Newfoundland, where eastbound convoys were assembling, Schneider found a number of likely targets, but he also found the Canadians to be very vigilant. After a number of near misses by destroyers and aircraft, Schneider thought it prudent to seek more sea room, and moved further out into the Atlantic. A few days later, he found Convoy SC 107 sailing straight towards his open torpedo tubes.

Schneider approached the convoy from the south, the ships of the outer starboard column being clearly visible in the light of the snowflakes still being fired by some of the more nervous merchant-men. With the *Empire Sunrise* gone, torpedoed four hours earlier by U-402, the starboard outer column consisted of the 2,130-ton Dutch timber carrier *Berkel* in the lead, followed by the British First World War veteran *Empire Lynx* and the Greek-flag *Mount Pelion*, another elderly steamer of 5,655 tons. They were all worthy targets, and beyond them lay row upon row of deep-laden ships, all steering a rigidly straight course and moving at the speed of a brewer's dray. Somewhere in the darkness, and not visible to Herbert Schneider, was the Canadian corvette *Arvida*, supposedly guarding the southern side of the convoy. Not that Schneider need have been too worried by the presence of the *Arvida*, her radar being out of action and her Asdic having a very limited range.

To aim at any specific ship would be irrelevant; Schneider simply emptied his bow tubes at the centre of the convoy and waited to see what harvest he would reap. Incredibly, three of U-522's four torpedoes missed, their tracks scything through the ranks of moving ships and disappearing into the night beyond. The fourth found a target.

J & C Harrison's 5,496-ton *Hartington*, carrying 8,000 tons of Canadian wheat, and with six Sherman tanks sitting incongruously on her hatch tops, was steaming in Column 7, a reasonably safe position in the opinion of Chief Engineer Archie Watson, who was then pacing her after deck. It was past midnight, but like most of those aboard the *Hartington* Watson had not slept that night. In his case partly due to the possibility of being torpedoed, but mainly out of concern for his engine.

The *Hartington* was not an old ship, having come out of her West Hartlepool yard in 1932, but she had a history of engine and boiler problems. She was fitted with a quadruple-expansion steam engine, as opposed to the triple-expansion engine favoured by most merchant steamers of her day. The extra cylinder called for higher steam pressures, which in turn led to boiler problems. Watson had lost count of the number of times *Hartington* had dropped out of various convoys through being unable to keep up speed. And tonight of all nights, with a U-boat pack gathering around them, he had good cause to worry.

Chief Engineer Watson's concerns did not stop with his engine. All was not right on the bridge of the *Hartington*. Captain Maurice Edwards was not a well man. Prior to sailing from the UK he had undergone a major operation from which he had not yet fully recovered. The Captain really should not have been at sea, but with so many ships going down, so many experienced men being lost, it was obvious that blind eyes had been turned.

Archibald Watson was no stranger to war, having lost his last ship, the *Harpasa*, only seven months earlier when she was bombed and set on fire by Japanese aircraft in the Bay of Bengal. He and his fellow survivors were picked up by the Indo China Navigation Company's *Taksang*, which in turn was then sunk. Thirty-nine of the *Harpasa* survivors were then lost with her. Prior to that, in April 1941, Watson had been torpedoed by U-107 in the *Harpathian* off the Azores. Now it was all about to happen again. Of that night in November 1942 he later wrote:

> The sea was calm, with light airs. There was no moon, and it was a very dark night, but visibility was good. No-one saw the track of the torpedo, which struck forward, between Nos 1 and 2 holds on the starboard side. There was a loud explosion and a flash, water and debris were thrown up over the bridge. The No. 1 hatches were blown off, some of which landed on the bridge. We carried two lifeboats, neither were damaged.

Five minutes after she was hit, the *Hartington* took a heavy list to starboard, and in anticipation that his ship might be about to capsize, Captain Edwards ordered his crew to lower the boats. Owing to the worsening list, some difficulty was experienced in launching the port boat, but, notwithstanding, the evacuation was carried out quickly and in an orderly manner. Ten minutes after the boats cleared the ship's side, the *Hartington* rolled over and sank bow first. At this juncture it appears that Chief Engineer Watson took charge of the boats. In his report he wrote:

> The boats closed, and I equally divided the survivors between the two boats. On making a roll call, we found that two men were missing. I am at a loss to know what happened to these men, as I saw them on the deck ready to abandon ship, and cannot understand why they were not in either lifeboat.

As the *Hartington*'s lifeboats dropped astern through the ranks of the convoy, they were hailed by HMCS *Restigouche* and also the Swedish ship *Pacific*, one of the rearguard of SC 107, so the survivors were confident that they would be picked up at daylight, or even before. With this in mind, they made no attempt to get under way, but drifted in the wake of the receding ships. They were shocked when at dawn they found themselves completely alone on an empty sea. After that, there was nothing they could do, except to wait out the day in the hope that someone would come back for them. At the time, the weather was fair, but in the afternoon it began to deteriorate. Soon, it was blowing a full gale, with rain squalls blotting out the horizon from time to time, and the two boats drifted apart.

Also in Chief Engineer Watson's boat were Captain Maurice Edwards and Second Officer George Joyce. Captain Edwards was too ill to take command, so it fell to Joyce and Watson to take joint charge. The weather relented during the night, and with no sign of rescue coming from the convoy, it was decided to make for New-foundland, then some 350 miles to the west, using the boat's engine and sails, if possible. The attempt to reach land was doomed to failure. Chief Engineer Watson's report gives details:

> The weather was fairly good for the first twenty-four hours, so I used the motor during the afternoon. A gale sprang up, making it impossible to sail, so we put out the sea anchor. The motor only functioned for a short time, and then broke down as the carbu-rettor and jets became fouled with salt. I could easily have cleaned them had there been any tools available, but the seas were too heavy for the motor to have been any use, so I did not waste energy in trying to put it in order. We lay to the sea anchor for a day till the painter broke. The boat then rode broadside on, and kept fairly dry. The gale continued for about six days, and when the wind dropped the swell remained extremely heavy, making rowing quite impossible. The rudder became unshipped every time it was left unattended, and with great difficulty I managed to ship it on two occasions, taking about an hour each time, but eventually had to give up trying, owing to the cold, and general weakness from exposure.

The unrelenting lurching of the boat in the swell, the lash of the spray coming over the gunwales, and above all the mind-numbing cold were taking a heavy toll of the twenty-four men crammed into the 28-foot lifeboat. Too make matters worse, Captain Edwards was now seriously ill. Morale began to plummet.

Spirits lifted again when, on their second day adrift, the survivors came across an abandoned lifeboat, evidently from another ship that had recently been torpedoed. Second Officer Joyce manoeuvred along-side the boat, and with the help of Chief Engineer Watson rescued a breaker of drinking water, a considerable amount of tinned corned beef, salmon and sardines, and a large tarpaulin. The food was a welcome addition to the rations their own boat carried, of which Watson said:

The new emergency food we carried was not at all popular; the pemmican made us thirsty, and the Horlicks milk tablets would not dissolve in our mouths, which were dry. It seems to me that these foods are satisfactory only when there is plenty of water ...

The acquisition of the tarpaulin proved to be heaven-sent, for with this the survivors rigged a cover over the whole length of the boat which protected them from the lash of the icy spray and rain squalls. Using the hand pump, the boat was kept reasonably dry, but even though they wore rubber survival suits, there was no keeping out the bitter cold, especially at night, when the temperature was near freezing.

With the boat made as comfortable as possible, a semblance of order was established, with Captain Edwards, who was beginning to regain his strength, taking control of food and water rationing, assisted by the Chief Steward and Third Engineer. Second Officer George Joyce, in overall charge, was a tower of strength. Of his efforts Chief Engineer Watson was later to say:

I cannot praise this officer too highly, as during the first days he spent long hours at the tiller in very bad weather, sometimes spending as much as twelve hours without relief, and it was undoubtedly due to his efforts that the boat was prevented from being swamped. Although seriously ill, on many occasions he crawled out from under the tarpaulin, exposing himself to the bitter elements, in order to study the wind and sea, and I hardly know how he managed to crawl back under cover again. Three days before we were picked up, Mr Joyce collapsed altogether from exhaustion, and no-one definitely took charge after this. Mr Joyce nearly paid with his life for his devotion to duty, and on landing he was so ill from exposure that he had to be forcibly fed, and was kept under continual medical observation day and night for some time.

On the condition of his fellow survivors, and in particular Third Engineer Frederick Young, Archie Watson commented:

Most of us had trouble with our feet, and the Captain's feet soon became very swollen and discoloured. The 3rd Engineer's feet also swelled and turned black after about five days. This officer was only wearing shoes, and his feet were probably wet most of the time. At one period he became delirious, which I think was caused by the excessive cold. He was an extremely good man in the lifeboat until he became too ill, and gave valuable assistance in rigging the canvas screens. He also made three tillers for the rudder and assisted in controlling the boat.

It was the opinion of Chief Engineer Watson that everyone in the boat 'behaved extremely well', which under the prevailing circumstances was praise indeed. Only one man did not survive that miserable voyage; he was 60-year-old ship's carpenter John Macrae, who died on the fourth day, probably from exposure. His body was committed to the deep with as much dignity as the weather would permit.

Deliverance came on 12 November, ten days after the *Hartington* was lost, in the form of the British destroyer *Winchelsea*, which was returning to St John's after escorting a convoy. It was by pure chance that she came upon the tiny lifeboat fighting its way to the west against the hostile sea. Of the *Hartington*'s other boat, under the command of Chief Officer Owen Clements, there was no news. The boat and its twenty-four occupants were never seen again.

As for the *Hartington* herself, she lived on for a few hours after Herbert Schneider's torpedo crippled her, abandoned and drifting aimlessly astern of the convoy. At 0206 on the 2nd, she was found by Rudolf Franzius in U-438. Franzius fired one torpedo, which went home, but still the *Hartington* did not sink. Another two hours went by before Klaus Bargsten in U-521 came along to deliver the *coup de grâce*.

U-521 was one of Dönitz's latest Type IXCs, commissioned in Hamburg at the beginning of June 1942 by Oberleutnant Klaus Bargsten. She was equipped with two supercharged M.A.N. diesels, which gave her a speed of 18.3 knots on the surface, and a range of 13,450 miles at 10 knots. She had spent some months working up in the Baltic, where she was attacked by several Russian submarines masquerading as U-boats. Fortunately for her, the Russians must have been in training, for all their torpedoes went wide, and U-521 escaped without damage.

On first venturing out into the Atlantic on her first war cruise, U-521 again ran into trouble. Sailing from Norway on 6 October 1942, she was passing to the north of Scotland when she was caught on the surface by a patrolling British aircraft, which swooped so low that her trailing antenna almost struck the U-boat's conning tower. For some reason, although the aircraft's bomb doors were open, no bombs were dropped. U-521 had taken refuge in the deep before the plane came round for a second attack.

There can be little doubt that much of U-521's apparent good fortune was due to the ability of 27-year-old Klaus Bargsten. Before joining the U-boats, he had been an officer with the North German Lloyd Line, serving mostly in their cargo ships, where he will have learned how to face up to extreme challenges. In his first command, U-563, he had already distinguished himself by torpedoing the Tribal-class destroyer HMS *Cossack* in a pack attack on Convoy HG 75. *Cossack* lost her commander and 158 men, but she was reboarded and taken in tow. Bad weather sank her three days later.

U-521 was a latecomer to the *Veilchen* pack, failing to make contact with SC 107 until the night of 1 November, when she sighted the abandoned *Hartington* straggling astern. Despite the presence of a corvette, Bargsten approached the *Hartington* on the surface and fired a torpedo from about 2,000 yards. This missed the merchantman and exploded close alongside the corvette, giving the impression that she had been hit. Bargsten then turned stern-on, and sank the *Hartington* with a torpedo from his stern tubes. Dawn was painting grey streaks in the sky to the east when the abandoned *Hartington* finally surrendered and took her cargo of grain and tanks to the bottom of the grey Atlantic.

Six weeks later, Navy chaplain J.M. Armstrong visited the *Hartington*'s survivors in hospital. He commented:

> The men in hospital told me they were adrift in an open boat for ten days, and were finally picked up when they had nearly succumbed to exposure. One of their number had perished. The story I had from these men was that the other boat, as far as they knew, had not been picked up. Three of the men in hospital have lost and are losing several of their toes. One of them is waiting until three of the toes of one foot drop off. He said that when that happened his recovery would probably be rapid. Another had had two taken off the morning of the day I last saw. Brave men these! They would have a go at it again if they could.

Another comment came many years later from the son of William Burgar, one of the *Hartington*'s DEMS gunners:

> At the time of the sinking Dad was off duty and he was wearing carpet slippers, and so had to keep his feet out of the icy cold

water that was swirling around the bottom of the lifeboat ...
Having carpet slippers turned out in the end to be good luck,
since every one else in the boat having boots, allowed their feet to
remain in the water. After rescue they were all found to be suffering from frostbite. The survivors were in a large hospital ward,
and each person had a cage over their feet to keep the weight of
the bedding off their feet. Dad says that on one day a surgeon
came along and lifted the bedding on each patient to inspect their
feet. He then went through the whole ward and removed toes
from many of the patients, with Dad having been one of the lucky
exceptions. However, he suffered for many years with poor feet,
but he was pleased to have kept his toes.

Gunner Burgar made a claim for compensation for his disability, but
this was refused on the grounds that, although he was a Royal Navy
rating, he was serving in a merchant ship and therefore the State was
not liable. Burgar fought, and eventually won his case. Ironically, he
was then awarded the British Empire Medal in recognition of his brave
conduct in the *Hartington*'s lifeboat.

CHAPTER FIVE

Crescendo

The sinking of the *Hartington* was the signal for some of the more nervous merchantmen to put on another display of pyrotechnics. Snowflakes went soaring high into the sky from all sides to burst overhead with spectacular brilliance. On that bitterly cold pre-dawn hour, they were hardly necessary. The moon was up, shining bright in a sky of broken cloud, and the shimmering Aurora Borealis was flambéing the sky to the north. The slow-moving ships were already silhouetted in stark relief against the horizon.

There was indeed real cause for concern. Only minutes before, HF/DF bearings taken by *Restigouche* and the *Stockport* had indicated that at least eight U-boats were in the vicinity of the convoy, confirming a signal received from the Admiralty. And yet, after the *Hartington* went down, the enemy appeared to have withdrawn.

Puzzled, but grateful for the lull, Commodore Watson and Lieutenant Commander Piers grasped the opportunity to regroup the convoy. Gaps left by the torpedoed ships were closed up and stragglers shepherded back into the fold, while in the darkness astern the rescue ships, *Stockport* and the two American tugs, watched over by the corvette *Celandine*, combed the sea for survivors. It was also time for mugs of steaming hot cocoa to be passed round, for lifejackets and duffel coats to be collected which had been left behind in the mad scramble when the alarm bells sounded, and for calls of nature to be answered. The guns remained fully manned, bridge watch keepers still swept the horizon with binoculars but, for the time being, at least, the pressure was off.

Surprisingly, it stayed that way for another three hours, giving those bearing the burden of command time to take stock, to mull over what had been done, and what had not been done. Under the circumstances, convoy discipline had been good, with no ship breaking ranks while under fire. But the consensus was that there had been a great deal of unnecessary use of snowflakes by some ships. Captain Willie Putt of the British steamer *Hatimura* later wrote:

I wish to complain about the indiscriminate firing of snowflake rockets during the attack on the convoy, as although we were given instructions at the convoy conference that they were not to be fired until orders were given, they were being fired continuously; the Americans especially seemed to be very keen on them. The whole convoy was illuminated, and could be seen for miles. I counted as many as eighty snowflakes in the air at one time.

Captain Arthur Hawkins of the abandoned *Empire Sunrise* was of a similar opinion, saying, 'I would like to protest against the continued firing of snowflakes by ships of this convoy, which I think gave the convoy away.' Captain Maurice Edwards of the *Hartington* agreed. 'As soon as this happened [the *Empire Sunrise* torpedoed] many ships in the convoy sent up snowflakes, causing the convoy to be brilliantly illuminated, making it a perfect target. These snowflakes were sent up continuously until we were sunk, and throughout the whole period it was as bright as day.'

The snowflake rocket, specifically designed for use by merchant ships, was set to explode at 1,200 feet, creating a brilliant white star of 300,000 candle power, which then floated down on a parachute. While the snowflake may have been without par as a distress signal, it was also, as illustrated above, a dangerous accessory in the hands of ships under fire.

In those unexpectedly quiet hours before the dawn, the sudden reappearance of the corvette *Moosejaw*, returning to C-4 Escort Group after repairs at St John's, was a welcome morale booster. For Lieutenant Commander Desmond Piers, who at this stage was growing ever more concerned for the safety of the ships under his protection, the arrival of the corvette was like manna from heaven. *Moosejaw* may have been only a glorified whaler, but she represented more guns, more depth charges, another stick with which to beat the enemy. Under the command of Temporary Lieutenant Lewis Quick, RCNR, she was well experienced in North Atlantic convoy work, and Piers stationed her in a key position on the port bow of the convoy. Then it was a case of waiting for the arrival of daylight, or whatever might come before that.

The wait was not a long one. Within half an hour of *Moosejaw* taking up her station the U-boats returned. Klaus Bargsten in U-521 led the way, closely followed by Hans-Joachim Hesse in U-442 and Horst Uphoff in U-84, who had some three hours earlier delivered the *coup de grâce* to the abandoned *Empire Sunrise*. The three-pronged attack brought the return of mayhem to SC 107.

Bargsten opened with a spread of three torpedoes aimed at the newly-arrived *Moosejaw*. Fortunately, the tracks were spotted by the corvette's lookouts, and Lieutenant Quick, true to his name, took instant avoiding action, turning under full helm to comb the tracks. Bargsten's torpedoes missed their intended victim, but it was a close shave, one torpedo skimming past *Moosejaw*'s stern with only feet to spare. U-84 followed, firing a brace of torpedoes at the ship nearest to her and U-442 joined in with four more fired at random.

In this free-for-all, the US tanker *L.V. Stanford*, in Column 6, reported a narrow miss, while the Armed Guard gunners aboard her fellow tanker *Tide Water*, in Column 5, were given the opportunity to practise their trade by firing at the torpedoes skimming past them.

The US Armed Guard were the American counterpart of the British DEMS gunners, only, as might be expected, on a much grander scale. Their numbers were greater, and the training more intense.

The United States Government, restricted by the Neutrality Act of 1936, was at first reluctant to arm merchant ships, and it was not until late in 1941, with America's involvement in the war imminent, that the guns and the men were forthcoming. From then on, typically, an American merchantman would be armed with a 5-inch stern gun, a 3-inch AA gun, eight 20mm cannons, and an assortment of light machine guns. The guns were manned and maintained by an Armed Guard comprising an officer, usually a US Navy ensign, twenty-four gunners and three communications specialists. The majority of these men were US Navy personnel, and were volunteers, the manning of a merchantman's guns being considered to be a 'hazardous assignment'.

Whereas in British merchant ships the Master decided when the guns were to be manned and fired, in American ships the Armed Guard officer had sole responsibility for defence, and acted independently. Inevitably, this state of affairs led to friction, for in any ship there can be only one commander. However, the system seemed to work, and the Armed Guard earned themselves a formidable reputation in the defence of their ships. This was amply illustrated by the gun action between the Liberty ship *Stephen Hopkins* and the German commerce raider *Stier*.

The 7,181-ton *Stephen Hopkins*, owned by the Luckenbach Steamship Company of New York, and commanded by Captain Paul Buck, was armed with a 4-inch stern gun, two quick-firing 37mm AA guns and six machine guns. The guns were manned by fourteen Armed Guard gunners under the command of Ensign Kenneth Willett. The ship was on a ballast voyage from Cape Town to Dutch Guiana when she crossed paths with the *Stier* in mid-Atlantic.

The *Stier*, an 18-knot ex-fruit carrier of the Deutsche Levant Line, was under the command of Kapitän-zur-See Horst Gerlach and manned entirely by trained naval men. She was armed with six 5.9-inch guns, two 37mm and four 20mm cannons, and two 21-inch torpedo tubes. She also carried two Arado spotter aircraft.

Refusing to surrender, Captain Buck turned stern-on to the raider and ran for the horizon, while his Armed Guard gunners fought a hopelessly one-sided duel; their single 4-inch against the *Stier*'s centrally controlled battery of 5.9s. Nevertheless, Ensign Willett and his gunners put thirty-five shells into the German raider, repeatedly hitting her below the waterline. Eventually, after a running battle that lasted most of the day, both ships were on fire and sinking, their decks littered with the dead and dying. Ensign Kenneth Willett died at his gun, as did most of his men.

Back with SC 107, U-442's randomly-aimed torpedoes had created bedlam, with ships firing at real and imaginary attackers, and once more the sky overhead was turned incandescent by brilliant white snowflakes. Neither the Senior Officer Escort nor the Convoy Commodore were able to exercise control over the mayhem, as their only means of instant communication with the merchant ships was by signal lamp or, as a last resort, by megaphone at close quarters. Under the circumstances prevailing, neither method was practicable. As for those manning the bridges of these ships, few had any clear idea of what was happening, and if there was momentary panic resulting in the indiscriminate firing of guns and rockets, then it was not surprising. The outcome was equally uncertain, but it was believed that U-442 was slightly damaged by machine gun fire from the corvette *Amherst*, and hit by a 3-inch shell, probably fired by the *Tide Water*.

When much of the commotion had died down, Siegfried von Forstner brought U-402 back to the surface, her torpedo tubes reloaded and primed ready to add to the chaos. She emerged between Columns 1 and 2, and von Forstner was immediately presented with a choice of targets, all conveniently backlit. He focused his sights on the 5,676-ton *Empire Leopard*, deep in the water, steering a straight course, and steaming at 7½ knots. And a sitting duck target in any U-boat commander's book.

Built in Seattle, on America's west coast, in 1917 for the US Shipping Board, the *Empire Leopard* had the distinction of being launched in record time – just sixty-seven days from keel to launch. Her pedigree was impeccable, but complicated. Originally named *War Flame*, she entered service with the US Navy as the USS *West Haven* and carried Army supplies to Europe during the First World War. She remained in Government service until January 1920, when she was decommissioned and sold to the Atlantic, Gulf & Pacific Steamship Company of Baltimore. In 1929, she passed to the Los Angeles Steamship Company, and was renamed *Marion Otis Chandler*. After nine years in the American coastal trade, she was bought by the Matson Navigation Company of San Francisco, and became the *Onomea*. When war broke out again in 1939, this much traded steamer, now a quarter of a century old, was acquired by the British Ministry of War Transport. Managed by Maritime Shipping & Trading of Cardiff, she then put to sea as the *Empire Leopard*, spending the next two years on the North Atlantic convoy run.

Under the command of Captain John Evan Evans, with a British crew of forty, the *Empire Leopard* had survived five round voyages between Britain and America, and was returning eastwards on what would be her twelfth crossing of the North Atlantic. She was carrying 7,410 tons of zinc concentrates, loaded in Botwood, Newfoundland, and consigned to Avonmouth. She had joined SC 107 off St John's on 29 October.

Zinc concentrates is an inert cargo, stowing at 20 cubic feet to the ton, with a buoyancy factor of nil, and liable to shift in heavy weather. It was not a cargo most experienced seamen would like to carry across the Atlantic in time of war.

Second Officer A. Crosby had the watch on the bridge of the *Empire Leopard* and was keeping his vigil in the starboard wing. The weather being fair and the visibility good, there was little for him to do but to stay alert and keep a close eye on the ship ahead. Three hours had passed quietly since the U-boats last attacked, and with the moon shedding a mellow light on the gently heaving sea, Crosby had time to think of other things, of home, of the time when there was no war. Like others in the convoy, he was even tempted to assume that the enemy had either lost contact with the convoy, or given up and moved on to other pastures.

The sudden return to reality was cruelly abrupt. There was a clap of thunder and the *Empire Leopard* staggered as Siegfried von Forstner's torpedo blew the bottom out of her. She took the hit in the port side of her engine room, her most vulnerable compartment. The sea poured in unchecked and the old Cardiff tramp took a heavy list, straightened up and then began to sink bodily, dragged down by the sheer deadweight of her ore cargo.

There was no time for niceties, for ringing alarm bells or firing rockets, and Second Officer Crosby, feeling the ship falling away from under his feet, made a dive for the ladder to the deck, his feet not touching the rungs as he slid down on the handrails. At the foot of the ladder he met Chief Officer Gordon Neil struggling into his lifejacket, then, as the two officers reached the lower bridge, Captain Evans joined them, and led the way to the boat deck. Crosby later wrote in his report of the sinking:

> ... before I could get to my boat station, and about twenty seconds after the torpedo struck us, the ship sank and I was taken down 20 feet below the water. The Chief Officer and Captain were not more than 5 feet away from me at the time, but I never saw either of them again.

The second miracle of the night came for Crosby when the sinking ship released her hold on him and he shot to the surface again. Just a few feet away, bobbing on the waves, was one of the *Empire Leopard*'s large wooden life rafts. Wasting no time, Crosby struck out for the raft, and when he dragged himself aboard found another survivor, an able seaman, was already there. Later, they were joined by another seaman, the Fourth Engineer, and an assistant steward. And after that, there were no more. The five men were all that remained of the *Empire Leopard*'s crew of forty-one. Captain Evans, Chief Officer Neil, Chief Engineer Ferguson, and all the other officers, along with sailors, firemen, stewards and cooks, all gone with the ship.

The lucky ones aboard the raft did not have to wait long for rescue. As soon as it was fully light, SC 107's rescue ship, the ex-cross Channel ferry *Stockport*, came along to pick them up. The voyage was still only four days old, and already her count of survivors rescued was mounting.

Chaplain Armstrong, sailing with HMCS *Restigouche*, later summed up the night:

> We were not to have the opportunity to get our heads down that night. At 0715Z/2 the convoy was attacked a third time. This time

the toll was the heaviest yet. Four more ships with their cargoes of inestimable value to our war effort were sent to the bottom. Each time a ship was torpedoed, every ship would send up snowflakes, illuminating the sky for miles around. But in spite of the illumination no sign of the skulking intruder was seen.

The long absence of any U-boat activity in the small hours of 2 November had been a welcome relief, an easing of the stress the men had been under for so long. Captain William Slade, on the bridge of the *Empire Antelope*, third ship of Column 2, and immediately astern of *Empire Leopard*, had not relaxed his vigilance, but was conscious that fatigue was slowing his reactions. He had not left the bridge since the first alarm some nine hours earlier, which would account for some of his tiredness, but this was only the culmination of twelve long months and eleven Atlantic crossings in convoy. All this time, U-boats apart, he had been nursing a 23-year-old ship which was showing worrying signs of ageing. Engine breakdowns were a common occurrence, necessitating repairs on reaching port on both sides of the Atlantic. The latest defect, in the steering gear this time, had been rectified in St John's, but it had been a rush job, leaving Slade with the nagging worry that the gear would fail again on the homeward passage.

The *Empire Antelope*, managed by the Moss Hutchinson Line of Liverpool for the Ministry of War Transport, was another ex-American ship, having started life in Tacoma, Washington as the *Ophis*, a 4,782-ton wartime replacement ship for the United States Shipping Board. Completed in August 1919, she was a 10-knot steamer built specifically for the Atlantic trade. In 1928, the US Shipping Board allocated her to the Colombian Steamship Company of New York, who renamed her *Bangu*. She spent the next nine years sailing between US East Coast ports and the Caribbean until, in 1937, she came under the control of the United States Maritime Commission, and was laid up as part of the reserve fleet.

In 1941, with Britain desperately short of merchant shipping, *Bangu* was sold to the Ministry of War Transport and became the *Empire Antelope*. Under the command of Captain William Slade she was quickly incorporated into the North Atlantic convoy round, carrying mostly cargoes of steel from the US and Canada. She and her British crew of fifty were an integral part of Britain's umbilical cord. Together, they had many nerve-wracking escapes, but none as humiliating as on her previous voyage with Convoy SC 94.

SC 94, an eastbound convoy of thirty-six ships, escorted by the Canadian C-1 Escort Group, consisting of a destroyer and five corvettes, suffered a devastating attack by a seventeen-strong U-boat pack in mid-Atlantic which lasted for five days and five nights. At the height of the attack, on the morning of 8 August, five ships were sunk in the space of two hours. They included the American steamer *Kaimoku*, which was carrying steel and a large quantity of ammunition. She was hit by a torpedo fired by Paul-Hugo Kettner in U-379.

When the U-boats attacked, only the British corvette *Primrose* was with the convoy, the other escorts all being astern chasing Asdic contacts. *Primrose* retaliated with depth charges, and while she was doing so a tremendous underwater explosion occurred, which was later put down to the *Kaimoku*'s ammunition exploding, probably set off by the corvette's depth charges.

So great was the explosion that ships in the immediate vicinity were thrown over on their beam ends. The crews of three – Ropner's *Empire Moonbeam*, the Cardiff tramp *Radchurch*, and the *Empire Antelope* – believing they had been torpedoed, promptly abandoned ship.

When the commotion had died down and it was realized that none of the three ships had been hit, rather shamefacedly, Captain Hewison of the *Empire Moonbeam* and Captain Slade of the *Empire Antelope* persuaded their men to reboard their ships and get under way again. Captain Lewin of the *Radchurch*, who had stayed behind with his ship, was unable to do the same. Despite the urgings of their officers, the *Radchurch*'s Lascar crew flatly refused to leave the boats and return aboard. The deserted tramp was left to drift astern of the convoy, where later in the day she was sunk by U-176.

In the circumstances prevailing, the behaviour of the crews of the three British ships might have been excused. Many of these men had been to hell and back, voyage after voyage, perhaps years, of Atlantic crossings in slow and poorly defended convoys, easy prey for Dönitz's U-boats. With their nerves stretched as tight as bowstrings they were constantly aware that, by the law of averages, it was only a matter of time before their ship was blown from under them. In truth, these men were 'torpedo happy' – and who could honestly blame them?

The men of the *Empire Moonbeam* and *Empire Antelope* did redeem themselves by reboarding their ships, but in the case of the *Radchurch* the refusal of her Lascar crew to go back was hard to excuse. Fortunately, this was the only such instance recorded in British merchant ships in the long war at sea.

For a few brief moments on that cold November morning in the North Atlantic, William Slade relived the humiliation of Convoy SC 94, then the stress of the past hours began to make itself felt. Suddenly, the thought of just a couple of hours rest snatched before the dawn became a temptation too hard to resist. He looked around him. The great ocean was quiet, with hardly a breath of wind to disturb its surface, the visibility was good, the clacking signal lamps were quiet, and the enemy appeared to have gone away. Handing over the bridge to Chief Officer Wilson, Captain Slade went below to his cabin. Unfortunately, he had misread the signs. He later wrote in his report to the Admiralty:

> I had only been below for a few minutes when at 0409 there was a loud explosion, the ship ahead of us, SS *Empire Leopard* was torpedoed on the port side and sank in 20 seconds. Before I could get out of my room, at 0410 Convoy Time on 2nd November, in position 52° 26′ N 45° 22′ W, we were struck by a torpedo on the port side in No. 3 deep tank amidships, just forward of the engine room. The explosion was not very loud, more of a dull thud, the ship shook violently, there was no flash but a column of water was thrown up to a considerable height, and a flame came up through the engineroom ventilator or boiler room. No one saw the submarine, nor the track of the torpedo.

Being close witness to the sudden and very violent end of the *Empire Leopard*, coupled with the shock of their own ship being torpedoed, might have sent the crew of the *Empire Antelope* into a blind panic. However, they were hardier men than the deserters of the *Radchurch*, and although this was 4 o'clock in the morning, an hour at which human life is said to be at its lowest ebb, they remained calm. Captain Slade's report continued:

> Hatch covers were blown off No. 3, both boats on the port side were destroyed, and the vessel immediately settled by the head on an even keel. When I reached the bridge the after starboard boat had been lowered and, owing to the weigh on the ship [*sic*.], the painter parted and the boat drifted rapidly astern with only ten men in her, without an Officer. The Chief Officer was on the boat deck attending to the lowering of the remaining starboard lifeboat, which was successfully lowered into the water. I returned to the bridge and threw all confidential books and papers overboard in weighted boxes. The bridge structure appeared to be intact, but

everything was in confusion so I could not find any rockets to fire the distress signal. The wireless set was also completely destroyed by the explosion, so no SSS message was sent out.

When the torpedo hit, the *Empire Antelope*'s Second Engineer, who was on watch in the engine room, immediately stopped the engine, but the ship had been steaming non-stop for three days, and she still carried a great deal of momentum. Consequently, when the starboard lifeboat hit the water, it was dragged along with the ship until the painter holding it alongside parted, and the boat, with only fourteen men on board, drifted astern into the night. This left twenty-six men, including Captain Slade, still on board the sinking ship with no life-boat. Captain Slade later reported on subsequent events:

> We released a raft and about eighteen men floated off on it in charge of the Chief Officer, then some of the gunners, who had stood by until the last, informed me that the large raft on the port side was jammed and they could not clear it. I got an axe, man-aged to cut the raft away, and the remaining eight of us left the ship on it. We then found that the bridle lashing on the raft had become foul, making it impossible to push the raft from the ship's side. I realised someone would have to reboard the vessel to cut the raft clear, and as I was the only one who knew anything about it, I waited until the raft lifted on the swell and scrambled back on deck. I chopped the raft clear, shouting to the men to keep as close alongside as possible, then I jumped for it, but missed the raft and fell in to the water. I was wearing my lifejacket, however, with the red light attached, and was quickly pulled on to the raft without further mishap. This being the weather side we had great diffi-culty in getting the raft away from the vessel. All the crew were clear within about 20 minutes of the ship being torpedoed.

All fifty crew members of the *Empire Antelope* had safely abandoned ship, despite the loss of one lifeboat, but the outlook for the twenty-six men clinging to the unprotected rafts was not good. The night air was cold, and with only a few inches between them and the sea they were constantly lashed by icy spray. The one lifeboat to get away came back and took on board as many as possible from the rafts, but in the end thirteen men, of which Captain Slade was one, were left to wait out the night on the rafts. At about 0530, as dawn approached, they watched their ship lift her stern high in the air, and plunge down bow-first into the depths. About two and a half hours later, all fifty men were picked up by the rescue ship *Stockport*, which already had over 200 survivors on board.

Shortly after he torpedoed the *Empire Antelope*, Siegfried von Forstner had been forced to dive when one of the escorts came to investigate. He brought U-402 back to the surface again at about 0530, just in time to see his latest victim take her last plunge and watch the *Stockport* take on board her survivors. Von Forstner was well pleased with his night's work, which amounted to four ships totalling nearly 20,000 tons sunk, and with the *Empire Sunrise* so badly damaged that she was easy meat for Uphoff in U-176. Now, von Forstner's torpedo tubes were empty, and he must go below to reload. This was a laborious process at sea, but with the weather holding good U-402 was back on the surface ready to attack again within three hours. Unfortunately, by this time the visibility had deteriorated, and all contact with the convoy was lost.

CHAPTER SIX

Reinforcements

For the Senior Officer Escort, Lieutenant Commander Piers, the torpedoing of the *Empire Antelope* was the culmination of a night of horror. In the space of seven hours he had lost six ships, first the *Empire Sunrise*, then the *Dalcroy*, the *Rinos*, the *Hartington*, the *Empire Leopard*, and now the *Empire Antelope*, nearly 33,000 tons of invaluable shipping, along with an as yet uncounted number of men, and over 40,000 tons of cargo. Piers was sorely missing his second destroyer. The corvettes were doing their best, but they were hopelessly outnumbered and outmanoeuvred by the enemy, then estimated to be seventeen strong. Furthermore, the Canadian corvettes were largely manned by inexperienced men, and all of them, including HMS *Celandine*, were too slow. The 18-knot U-boats were literally running rings around them. Air cover had been sporadic, mostly non-existent, and with the 600-mile-wide air gap drawing near, even that would soon end. The only one small hope lay with the weather. The North Atlantic, unbelievably quiet for so long, was at last beginning to show its teeth. The sky was clouding over and the wind and sea were rising, all of which foretold of a deterioration in visibility. SC 107 desperately needed some fog or rain squalls to hide in, but for the moment its ships were cruelly exposed.

While U-402 had been busy creating havoc on the port side of the convoy, Herbert Schneider, in U-522, having temporarily lost contact after sinking the *Hartington*, was stealthily approaching from the south. The Canadian corvette *Arvida* was guarding the starboard quarter of SC 107, but her radar, not for the first time, was out of action, and she was unaware of the threat. This left Schneider free to move in close to the massed merchantmen. Without bothering to take aim, he fired a spread of four torpedoes at the outer column, and then sheered away back into the darkness.

The unlucky recipient of one of Schneider's torpedoes was the British-flagged steamer *Maritima*, which had only recently, on orders from the Convoy Commodore, moved in to take the place of the *Empire Sunrise* in the starboard outer column.

The 5,801-ton *Maritima* was in her thirty-first year, her keel having first tasted salt water as far back as 1912, just a few months after the mighty *Titanic* met her iceberg off the Grand Banks. She had begun her long career as the *Port Lincoln*, a cargo/passenger vessel owned by the Commonwealth & Dominion Line of London. In 1927 she passed into the hands of the William Thomas Shipping Company of Liverpool, and was renamed *Cambrian Baroness*. Three years later, she changed names again, becoming the *Clan Graham* of Clan Line Steamers. Finally, in 1938, she ended up with Neil & Pandelis, Greek-owned but registered in London as the *Maritima*.

Despite her great age, the *Maritima*, stoutly built in a North East shipyard, and well-maintained, was still a smart ship, although the 13 knots she had once been capable of was now only her chief engineer's pipe dream. Loaded to her winter marks with 7,000 tons of assorted military cargo, she was sorely pressed to keep pace with the other ships as they inched their way through U-boat infested waters.

On the *Maritima*'s bridge, 66-year-old Captain Arthur Phelps-Mead, one of the old school of shipmasters, was displaying his customary *sang-froid*, but at the same time was uncomfortably conscious of the large consignment of explosives he carried in his tween decks. He was reluctant to leave the bridge, even though the watch was in the capable hands of Chief Officer Lamont and Second Officer Gibson. Also on the bridge were the First Radio Officer, the helmsman, and two DEMS gunners standing by the Oerlikons in the wings.

Captain Phelps-Mead's fears were realized when, at 0415, one of Herbert Schneider's randomly aimed torpedoes found its mark in the *Maritima*'s hull. Chief Officer Lamont described the sequence of events that followed:

> The torpedo struck the ship between No. 2 and 3 hatch, a little before the bridge, with a very loud explosion. I saw no flash or flame, but a huge column of water and smoke was thrown up, and the ship took a heavy list to starboard. I was on the bridge with the Master, the 2nd Officer, and Radio Officer, but could not see the extent of the damage, as it was very dark, but I did see both starboard boats flung into the air in pieces.
>
> The engines stopped immediately, we hoisted the red light, and fired rockets, then the Master ordered abandon ship. We got the port forward boat away in about two minutes. It was already swung out, so we had only to release the gripes. In lowering this

boat, the forward fall was let go and the boat fell bow first and swamped, but we were able to bail it out. I am not quite sure what happened to the port after boat, but I know that it capsized after being lowered, as I picked up the 2nd Engineer and Bosun who were hanging on to the keel of this boat. I went down from the bridge on to the port side, and the Captain went down on the starboard side, and I never saw him again. Nine men succeeded in getting away on a raft from the port side.

Clearing the ship's side, Lamont stood off and watched the *Maritima* go down. Within an estimated five minutes of being torpedoed, she rolled over to starboard, broke in two and sank. Lamont had a crew of twelve men in his boat, which was completely waterlogged. The oars were manned, and five more survivors were pulled from the water. One of the ship's wooden life-rafts was also sighted, and was found to have nine more men on board. They appeared to be safe, so Lamont left them on the raft. The lifeboat crew then set about bailing out the boat, and as they were doing so, the throb of diesel engines was heard nearby. A large submarine, most probably U-522, then appeared out of the night, and for one heart-stopping moment he feared that they were about to be taken prisoner. However, the U-boat had other business. Lamont later remarked: 'The submarine, which appeared to be a big one of about 1,000 tons, passed between the lifeboat and the raft, steaming west at about 18 knots, but it did not interfere with either.'

Lamont decided his best chance of rescue lay with holding the lifeboat in the vicinity of the sinking, which with the wind strengthening and the sea becoming rougher, was not easy. He and his fellow survivors spent a very uncomfortable four hours until, when it was fully light, they were picked up by HMCS *Arvida*. The corvette also found the drifting life-raft and took off the nine men on board. The twenty-seven men rescued were all that remained of the *Maritima*'s crew of fifty-nine. The remaining thirty-two, including Captain Phelps-Mead and Chief Engineer Thomas Rennie, had gone down with their ship.

Two of Herbert Schneider's torpedoes were wasted, passing between the lines of ships to disappear into the night on the other side of the convoy. The remaining torpedo found a target in the hull of the Greek steamer *Mount Pelion*, stationed directly ahead of the *Maritima*.

The 5,655-ton *Mount Pelion* was another elderly cosmopolitan, having been built in the Kawasaki Dockyard at Kobe in 1917, and subsequently serving under three flags. She began life as the *War Prince*, under the management of Furness, Withy & Company, Liverpool, was sold to the French shipowners Messageries Maritimes in 1920, and eventually ended up in the hands of Elias G. Culucundis & Stephen C. Costomeni of Athens.

With a total complement of thirty-nine on board, the *Mount Pelion* was carrying 7,452 tons of military stores, including motorized transport, when Schneider's torpedo exploded deep in her bowels. With her back broken, she went down with dignity, allowing all but seven of her crew to take to the boats. The hard-worked *Stockport* was there to pick up the survivors. The rescue ship, along with the tugs *Pessacus* and *Uncas*, had worked ceaselessly through the night, and between them they now had a total of 250 survivors on board.

When daylight finally came on the 2nd, the cloud was at mast-top height and depositing a miserable mixture of cold drizzle and mist. The wind had risen, and the white horses were running. The only ray of sunshine to brighten the miserable morning had been the unexpected arrival of the corvette HMCS *Moosejaw*. Assigned for duties with Operation Torch in the Mediterranean, she was joining SC 107 for the Atlantic crossing in answer to Lieutenant Commander Piers' frantic calls for help.

Commanded by Temporary Lieutenant Lewis Quick, *Moosejaw* had recently suffered two serious groundings that had kept her in port under repair for several months. She was also, like all the Canadian Flower Class corvettes, slow and poorly equipped, but to Piers she was heaven-sent, another arrow in his quiver with which to fend off the rampaging U-boats.

When she made her hurried departure from St John's, *Moosejaw* was three men short of her full complement, and those that were on board were mostly raw recruits who had never even seen the sea before. The majority of these unfortunate men were stricken with sea-sickness for the first four days at sea. It fell to the corvette's officers to sail the ship – and some of them were suffering in a similar manner.

After all the excitement had died down, Lieutenant Commander Piers rearranged his escorts. The outer screen consisted of *Celandine* ahead, *Amherst* on the port quarter, and *Arvida* to starboard, while closer in *Restigouche* was just ahead of the leading ships, with *Moosejaw* and *Algoma* on the port and starboard bows respectively. With the still meagre force Piers now had at his disposal it was good cover.

Unfortunately, soon after the escorts were in place both *Celandine* and *Arvida* reported their radars out of action. The loss of *Arvida*'s outdated Type SW was not significant, but with visibility falling *Celandine*'s Type 271 would be sorely missed.

SC 107 was now 420 miles north-east of St John's and was theoretically still within range of air cover from the RCAF base at Torbay, Newfoundland, but none was forthcoming. This may have been due to the low cloud and poor visibility, the latter the more likely, for the Torbay airfield, built in 1941, was in an area plagued by sea fog.

In 1942, the Royal Canadian Air Force, much like Canada's Navy, was short of trained personnel. Additionally, the few long-range aircraft it possessed were inadequate for work with the Atlantic convoys. Based at Torbay were a handful of Catalina amphibious flying boats, and a few Lockheed Hudson and Douglas Digby bombers. While these were all proven American-built aircraft, they lacked the range to reach out into the Atlantic to cover convoys when they were at their most vulnerable. Of the three aircraft, the Catalina, or Canso as the Canadians renamed it, had a there-and-back range of 2,500 miles, and carried a 1,000lb bomb load, but its maximum speed was only 196mph. Given fair warning by its lookouts a U-boat on the surface was easily able to dive before the Catalina was close enough to attack. What the RCAF really needed to protect the convoys were the big four-engined B-24 Liberators. Classed as a Very Long Range bomber, the Liberator was armed with ten .50 calibre machine guns, carried a 2,700lb bomb load, had a maximum speed of 290mph, and a one-way range of 1,800 miles. Not unexpectedly, the relatively new Liberator was in short supply, and the RCAF was at the back of the queue behind the USAAF and the RAF.

As the day progressed, the weather deteriorated further, and for a while it seemed that the U-boats had lost contact with SC 107. Not so Herbert Schneider in U-522. After sinking the *Maritima* and the *Mount Pelion*, he had been following close astern of the convoy. At 1443, he fired two torpedoes at the rear ship of Column 8.

The 3,189-ton *Parthenon* was even longer in the tooth than her fellow Greek, the recently foundered *Mount Pelion*. A product of West Hartlepool, and currently owned by Pithis Brothers & Co of Chios, she first went to sea in 1908 as the *Fameliaris*. She was rechristened *Ambatielos* in 1915, became the *P.L.M. 7* in 1917, and was acquired by the Pithis Brothers in 1922.

One of Schneider's torpedoes was sufficient to blast open the *Parthenon's* thinning plates, and she settled slowly, giving most of her crew ample time to take to the boats. Six men had been killed by the exploding torpedo, the remaining twenty-three, including Captain Nikolaos Kostalas, were rescued by the *Stockport*, which was nearby. In manoeuvring to pick up the survivors the *Stockport* almost came to grief when she struck an abandoned steel lifeboat with her propeller. The collision was sufficient to momentarily stop the rescue ship's engines, but fortunately she suffered no serious damage.

Restigouche and *Arvida* also came to the *Parthenon's* aid, but although *Arvida* obtained a doubtful Asdic contact and dropped depth charges, U-522 was by then already well clear and going deep.

The remainder of the day was quiet, and the convoy moved steadily eastwards in falling visibility. When, at about 1830, the sun slipped below the horizon and the temperature plummeted, the mist thickened into a typical Grand Banks fog, dense and persistent. This was the nightmare situation that both Lieutenant Commander Piers and Commodore Watson feared – thirty-three merchantmen, none of which was equipped with radar, steaming blind in close proximity to each other, was a recipe for disaster. Dimmed stern lights were used, but even with a lookout posted right forward in the eyes of the ship, the sighting of a half-power stern light on the ship ahead was often too late to avoid a collision. Consequently, ships instinctively dropped back until, eventually, the convoy was strung out over a distance of 4 miles. To add to the confusion, the funnel of the only motor vessel in the convoy, the US Navy supply ship *Pleiades*, caught fire, and some ships scattered, believing another attack to be under way.

Captain Stevens, Master of the commodore ship *Jeypore* reported:

Early in the morning of 3rd November the funnel of the US *Pleiades*, a diesel electric ship, caught fire and the blaze could be seen from 20 miles. The Vice Commodore's ship, thinking the U-boats were bound to see the flame from this ship, hoisted two red 'Not Under Command' lights and fell out of the convoy and at 0130 the convoy seemed to split into two parties. We carried on and at daylight on the 3rd November Nos 4, 3, 2 and 1 columns were about 5 or 6 miles astern of the convoy and to the westward. We reduced speed half a knot to allow them to catch up. At 0800 the U-boats began attacking again, and an American tanker, I think No.74, was torpedoed. At 0900 I spotted two torpedoes crossing the bow of the *Hatimura* and a minute later a third torpedo track coming straight for my ship. I went full speed ahead (11 knots) and hard aport, the torpedo missed me and ran ahead of the convoy.

Fortunately, the *Veilchen* U-boats were also disorganized, and no serious attack developed. However, the numerous HF/DF reports still being received by *Restigouche* and *Stockport* indicated that they had not gone away. Then, without warning, SC 107's abysmal outlook began to change. At about 0030 on the 3rd, *Restigouche* was 6 miles astern investigating an HF/DF report, when a radar contact was obtained on the port bow at 500 yards. At first, it was thought to be a U-boat on the surface, and *Restigouche* went in to attack, only to discover at the last minute that the radar echo was in fact HMS *Vanessa*.

Vanessa, a 1918-vintage Admiralty 'V' class destroyer, which had somehow found the convoy despite the poor visibility, had been detached from Convoy HX 213 to reinforce SC 107's defences. Twice bombed by enemy aircraft, sustaining heavy damage on both occasions, *Vanessa* had only recently returned to the North Atlantic. Although she was no longer young, she carried four quick-firing 4-inch guns and a substantial complement of depth charges and, above all, she was still capable of 34 knots, exactly what Lieutenant Commander Piers needed in his prolonged battle with the U-boats.

Towards dawn, the visibility began to improve, and soon ships were visible to each other at up to 3,000 yards. This was a manageable distance, and before long Commodore Watson had returned the convoy to a reasonable semblance of order. Back in their columns, and with six escorts, including two destroyers, forming a screen around them, it seemed that the merchantmen had a good chance of survival. Then the U-boats came back in force.

The American tanker *L.V. Stanford*, second ship of Column 6, was first to raise the alarm, reporting being narrowly missed by two torpedoes. Then the gunners aboard a second US tanker, the *Tidewater*, in the adjacent column, opened fire on the track of another torpedo as it sped past their ship. Five minutes later, two more torpedoes shot across the *Tidewater*'s stern. At least three of these randomly aimed torpedoes emanated from the bow tubes of Klaus Bargsten's U-521, one of them eventually striking yet another American oil carrier, the *Hahira*, in Column 8.

The *Hahira*, a 6,885-ton steam tanker owned by the Atlantic Refining Company of Philadelphia, was on passage from New York to an unspecified British port with 8,985 tons of fuel oil. She was under the command of Captain James Elliot, and carried a crew of thirty-eight and eighteen US Navy Armed Guards.

At approximately 0839 on 3 November, lookouts aboard the *Hahira* reported seeing the tracks of two torpedoes, one of which passed ahead of the ship, the other close astern. The *Hahira* had been well and truly bracketed, and Bargsten's third torpedo did not miss, exploding in the tanker's aftermost cargo tank.

Captain Stevens of the *Jeypore* reported:

At 1130 I heard a lot of firing in the centre of the convoy. It appeared to come from an American ship, and I imagine she was firing at a supposed torpedo. Anyway, the angle of fire was such that I had to duck as the shells whistled over the bridge. The US *Pleiades* thinking the shells bursting in the water were the tracks of torpedoes immediately opened fire on them but after a short time the firing ceased and the convoy continued quietly.

Captain Putt, on the bridge of the *Hatimura*, was another witness to the pandemonium that was breaking out:

On the morning of 3rd November, just before 1100, I saw a torpedo approaching from the starboard side, but was able to evade it by putting the helm hard over to port, and the torpedo just cleared my bow. Three more torpedoes were fired directly after two of which passed my bow by a good bit further ahead, and one struck a tanker, No. 73 in the convoy, which sank at 1100. We could just see the tracks of all these four torpedoes which ran through the water just breaking the surface, making a high pitched whistling sound.

The torpedo which struck the *Hahira* almost completely destroyed her stern section, and blazing oil spewed out onto her decks and accommodation. Fortunately, although the *Hahira* was 22 years old, she was fitted with a modern fire smothering system, which held the raging flames at bay long enough for Captain Elliot and fifty-five of his crew to get away in the boats.

The sinking of the *Hahira* was only the start of a bad day for SC 107. As the shadows lengthened and darkness closed around Convoy SC 107 on 3 November, Lieutenant Commander Piers had fears for the coming night, and these he expressed in his report to the Admiralty:

Shortly after this attack the weather cleared into a cloudless sky with brilliant sunshine. The eagerly awaited air support failed to arrive and my 1431Z/3 was made. The forenoon might be described as 'extremely active'. HMCS *Amherst* sighted a U-boat on the horizon on the port bow and went off in pursuit. HMS *Celandine*, 15 miles astern after having lost touch during the night, attacked a U-boat sighted on the surface and subsequently was attacked by torpedoes. HMCS *Restigouche* counter-attacked a doubtful contact with two charges ahead of Column 8 at 1342Z. Forty-four minutes later a periscope was sighted in between the third and fourth columns. Most ships in the convoy blazed away with every gun they had. Being thus surrounded by U-boats it was considered dangerous to carry out operation 'Artichoke' and thus leave the whole van unprotected, so *Restigouche* was the only ship to investigate the possible periscope. No definite information could be obtained, and the search was without result. No attack was made and the fact of the sighting is doubted.

The number of HF/DF bearings obtained during the day was forewarning of what was to come later. Without sufficient escorts to investigate and no air support, the convoy was in for a bad night. Bold evasive turns were made, but the clear visibility nullified their power of deception. As Rescue Ship *Stockport* was loaded to capacity with survivors, US tugs *Pessacus* and *Uncas* were detailed to act as rescue ships.

Lieutenant Commander Piers was fully justified in calling for air support, as SC 107 was still just within range of the Newfoundland airfields, but again no help was forthcoming.

Unfortunately, the SOE's assumption that the convoy was surrounded by U-boats was all too correct. In fact nine U-boats were now in contact with SC 107, and waiting the opportunity to strike. This was confirmed by Dönitz's war diary for 3 November, which names the boats as U-71 (Hardo Rodler von Roithberg), U-84 (Horst Uphoff), U-381 (Wilhelm-Heinrich Graf Pückler und Limpurg), U-402 (Siegfried Freiherr von Forstner), U-438 (Rudolf Franzius), U-521 (Klaus Bargsten), U-522 (Herbert Schneider), U-571 (Helmut Möhlmann) and U-704 (Horst Wilhelm Kessler).

Three men had been lost when the US tanker *Hahira* was torpedoed, two crewmen and one gunner, who were most probably killed by the explosion. The fifty-five survivors were picked up within forty-five minutes by the *Stockport*, which brought her total of survivors on board up to 350, three times what she was equipped to carry. At this point Lieutenant Commander Piers ordered the Iceland-bound harbour tugs to take over as rescue ships, advising them to show their steaming lights at night to avoid being mistaken for U-boats.

There was an unhappy sequel to the rescue. When the *Stockport* landed the *Hahira* survivors in Reykjavik, fourteen of them opted to be repatriated to the United States on the first suitable ship. They embarked on the *Parismina*, a cargo/passenger vessel owned by the United Fruit Steamship Company of New York, sailing from Reykjavik on 13 November.

The *Parismina*, commanded by Captain Edward T. Davidson, another veteran steamer launched at the turn of the century, was bound for Boston, Massachusetts with 200 tons of sand ballast, a crew of forty-eight, twelve Armed Guard gunners, and the *Hahira* survivors travelling as passengers. She joined the New York-bound convoy ONS 144 as it passed south of Iceland.

ONS 144 was made up of a collection of superannuated merchant-men steaming in nine columns at the unbelievably suicidal speed of 6 knots and escorted by one British and four Norwegian corvettes. This convoy was a gift to the U-boats, and should never have been allowed to put to sea in the North Atlantic. In anticipation of what might come to pass, ONS 144 was supported by the British rescue ship *Perth*.

The convoy was sighted on the 15th by Klaus Bargsten in U-521, then on his way to the Mediterranean. What followed was almost a carbon copy of the savaging of SC 107, and further demonstrated how the U-boats were running riot in the North Atlantic. Dönitz gathered together a thirteen-strong pack named *Kreuzotter* (Adder), which then homed in on Bargsten's signals.

The opening attack, by U-521 on the night of the 15th, was a complete failure. Bargsten penetrated the escort screen without difficulty and fired three salvos of torpedoes, all of which missed their targets. It was not until the rest of the pack arrived, after dark on the 17th that the battle began in earnest. First to go down, torpedoed by U-264, was the Greek steamer *Mount Taurus*. The small British ship *Widestone* was next, falling to U-184. Then, in the early hours of the 18th, the British tanker *President Sergent* was hit by U-624, which then went on to cripple the American freighter *Yaka* and sink the *Parismina*. Bill Adams of the US Maritime Service Veterans described the loss of the *Parismina*:

The *Parismina* sank in only four minutes following the torpedo's hit at 5.06am. At the time of the attack, the ship was in ballast, with nothing to cushion the explosion, which came on the starboard side between No. 2 hold and midships. *Parismina* settled by the bow, and sank at 5.10am, in rough seas, with a fire in the forward area.

The crew attempted to launch lifeboats and rafts, but while No. 2 boat was being lowered, the after falls were let go, throwing those in the boat into the water. Then the boat itself fell on top of its dumped group of souls, who were struggling in the frigid water. Master Edward T. Davidson was in the water, holding on to the rudder of No. 3 boat. Two men in that boat moved him around to the port side. Unable to lift him, they tied him to the boat. He died of exposure.

Lifeboat No. 4 filled with water, and men died in this boat from exposure. Because the ship was part of a convoy, fifty-four people who had been on the *Parismina* were picked up by the British rescue ship *Perth* and one survivor was found by HMS *Rose*.

The *Parismina* had been sunk by Ulrich Graf von Soden-Fraunhofen in U-624. One minute later, he torpedoed the Norwegian corvette *Montbretia* which had given chase to U-624. Thorlief Tobiassen, Able Seaman on board the corvette *Potentilla*, was an eyewitness:

In the engagement which followed it appears that the corvette passed between two submerged U-boats and was hit at 6 o'clock by a torpedo in the starboard bow. A gaping hole appeared in the bow and the forecastle deck twisted upwards. All the ammo and the 4-inch gun platform exploded sending a hail of red-hot metal over the after deck killing three men. The roof of the asdic deck came down. The bridge distorted and the bulkheads in the wheelhouse stowed in, killing the helmsman. The CO now gave order to abandon ship and three carleys were launched when the second torpedo struck in the boiler room, port side. The corvette now more or less fell apart and went down with forty-seven men ... two carleys and a cork net with men on them were sighted at 9 o'clock and the *Potentilla*'s whaler was manned and pulled over towards the cork net while *Potentilla* approached the carleys, from which twenty men were rescued, and five from the cork net. Some were badly injured, two of whom later died and were buried at sea that same afternoon. Earlier that morning *Potentilla* had also spotted a number of red lights in the water, and a man was seen trying to hold another man above water. One of *Potentilla*'s depth charge crew grabbed a line and was about to jump in to save them when the engine room telegraph rang 'Full speed ahead' and he had to leave them.

CHAPTER SEVEN

Commodore Down

The shock of the sinking of *Veilchen*'s latest victim, the American tanker *Hahira*, had worn off by the time the sun was over the yardarm on the 3rd. The weather continued fine, clear and cold with a light north-westerly, and so it would be for the rest of the day. The remaining ships of the convoy had closed ranks, and with the seven escorts of C-4 Group maintaining a tight screen around the merchantmen, the U-boats appeared content to keep their distance. By the time the sun went down at about 4 o'clock that afternoon, and darkness began to close in, an almost perceptible air of quiet confidence had settled over the convoy. The generally unspoken opinion in the ships was that if they could make it through the night, then, with less than thirty-six hours steaming before they came within range of Coastal Command's Liberators based on Iceland, they were home and dry. Simplistic, overly optimistic perhaps, but for men who had lived with violent death for five days and nights, it was something to hold on to.

In the short twilight that followed the sunset, on the bridge of SC 107's commodore ship, British India's *Jeypore*, Captain Thomas Stevens took time to reflect on what for him had not been the best of voyages. Sailing from London early in the previous January, the *Jeypore* had embarked on her usual itinerary, a long haul around the Cape, calling at South and East African ports to discharge, then north to load tea and jute for the homeward voyage. For the *Jeypore*'s Lascar crew of eighty-three, arrival in India would be the culmination of two years in the ship, and by law they would then be free to return to their villages, to their homes and families. They were counting the days.

Having completed her African coast discharge, the *Jeypore* returned to Durban to take on bunkers, arriving on 20 June. The first man aboard when she docked was the Admiralty's Sea Transport Officer, who informed Captain Stevens that his ship was urgently required on the far side of the Atlantic. India had been cancelled, and on completion of bunkering the *Jeypore* was to retrace her steps around the Cape, sail north-west to Trinidad, then north to New York, where she would load Admiralty cargo for British ports. This was not an unpleasant surprise for Stevens and his officers, as they had not been looking forward to India in the grip of the damp and miserable South-West Monsoon. The warm Caribbean, followed by the bright lights of New York, then home, had much more appeal. For the *Jeypore*'s Lascar crew, however, it was bad news, meaning another seven or eight months at sea, much of it in U-boat infested waters. The Lascars were furious to the point of mutiny. Seaman Gunner Thomas Buck, one of the ten DEMS gunners in the ship, relates what followed:

> They immediately went on strike and threatened to leave the ship. The Master of the ship, Captain Thomas Stevens, had the task of explaining this to the crew and asked them to wait until he had the chance to talk to the Admiralty before acting. He told his 1st Officer to explain this to the other officers and gun crews, and our orders were on no account was anyone allowed to leave the ship. For a period of time this was obeyed but we didn't know that they were preparing for a battle, making weapons of sharpened bamboo sticks to force us to let them leave. Then all hell broke out, they all came out together, placed bags of flour or rice on the deck to hide behind and there was just eight of us lining the deck, which was about 3 foot high, and we were in the thick of it. I stopped a blow on the head, which was cut but not serious enough to stop me and the fighting lasted for some time, until one of the officers, who were on the upper deck, told the other two gunners to get a marlin gun and fire into the stack of bags of flour or rice that were on the hatch on the lower deck. This was carried out and had an immediate impact. They all ran for cover. Then the police arrived on the scene in force and arrested all the crew. None of the crew showed any sign of injury. We were all later summoned to attend court, but I was the only casualty who went in. Some of the crew turned up in bandages saying they had been injured, but the prosecuting lawyer had the bandages removed to reveal no injuries! After a lot of talking it was settled in a very short time with all the crew being sent to prison. All this trouble, as far as we were concerned, gave us a lovely time in Durban, God's gift to paradise. It's a wonderful place and I shall never forget the hospitality.

With a new crew on board, the *Jeypore* finally left Durban on 6 August, after nearly seven weeks in port. She reached Trinidad a month later, and then went by coastal convoy to New York. After loading a cargo which included the customary parcel of explosives, she joined Convoy SC 107 for the Atlantic crossing.

U-89 was another latecomer to Group *Veilchen*. As she approached SC 107 after dark on 3 November, Kapitänleutnant Dietrich Lohmann was also reflecting on past events.

Lohmann, aged 33, had commissioned U-89 in Lübeck in the late autumn of 1941, and was now on his second war patrol in command. Her maiden voyage had taken her to America's east coast to join in Admiral Dönitz's highly successful Operation Drumbeat, where Lohmann suffered the most cruel run of bad luck. In a patrol lasting seventy-seven days he logged only one success, that being the sinking by gunfire of the 54-ton Canadian trawler *Lucille M*. Then, crossing the Bay of Biscay when homeward bound from this unrewarding venture, U-89 was pounced upon by Liberator F/120, piloted by Squadron Leader Terrence 'Bull' Bulloch. Sergeant B. Turnbull, a pilot flying with Bulloch under training, later wrote the following account of the incident:

> I was sitting in Bull's seat and was first to sight this U-boat at about 8 miles to starboard. I called to Bull and we swopped places. During the first attack with depth charges I was standing in the bomb bay. It wasn't until a year later that U-boats were instructed to stay on top and fight it out, so our drill was to head for the U-boat as quickly as possible, because as soon as he saw us he'd dive and would submerge in 45 seconds.
>
> As there was nothing for me to do on the flight deck I got out of the road and decided to make myself useful by dropping an aluminium sea marker. Bull increased the revs, opened the throttles and stuffed the nose down so for a minute or so we had a pretty bumpy ride. I'd got halfway through the bomb bays on my return forward with the sea marker in one hand when I heard the click of the bomb door release. I dropped the marker and grabbed a pillar with my hand. My feet were firmly on the narrow duck walk (14 inches at the top and 10 inches at the bottom). As the doors ran up the side of the fuselage the noise was deafening and the draught so strong that I had some doubt whether I'd be able to hang on. Later experience showed that we must have been doing more than 200 knots. The sea looked very close and cold. The depth charges rolled from their racks down the pillars, squeezing my fingers on the way past, but I was near enough welded to the

outfit by then. The U-boat went past in an instant blur and we climbed away. The noise from the engines and the wind and the cannons had left me pretty deaf, but as the bomb doors slowly closed shut the relief was much appreciated and the hair on the back of my neck returned to normal.

Reports of the damage inflicted on U-89 by Bulloch's Liberator are conflicting, but as she had only reached a depth of 10 metres when the depth bombs exploded close around her, it must have been more than superficial. The U-boat reached port safely, but she had not seen the last of Squadron Leader 'Bull' Bulloch and his Liberator.

Running on the surface, but with U-89 trimmed down so that her casings were only just clear of the water, Dietrich Lohmann crept past SC 107 on its starboard side and pulled ahead for several miles. The massed ships of the convoy were backlit by the glow of the Northern Lights, and showing in clear silhouette. Lohmann had only to heave to and wait for them to steam into his sights.

At 1753, Lohmann fired a full spread of four torpedoes from his bow tubes. First in his line of fire was the 1,712-ton *Titus*, owned by the Royal Netherlands Steamship Company of Amsterdam. In more peaceful times a short-sea trader more at home in the Mediterranean than the wide Atlantic, the *Titus* was carrying a cargo of flour from Halifax. Two of Lohmann's torpedoes narrowly missed her, exploding prematurely dangerously close to her hull. The blast was so fierce that the little Dutch ship was lifted clean out of the water, and rolled onto her beam ends, before righting herself. Her crew, convinced they had been torpedoed, lowered their lifeboats and abandoned ship. Their actions showed that, even after ten hours had passed without an attack, nerves were still stretched to breaking point.

Lohmann's other torpedoes carried on into the convoy, one of them on a collision course with the Convoy Commodore's ship the *Jeypore*. Captain Tom Stevens later wrote of the loss of his command:

> The 3rd Officer reported sighting the track of the torpedo which was then about 20 yards off the ship, about 2 pts before the beam, and it was too late to alter course. Immediately upon impact there was a terrific explosion. The torpedo struck in the bulkhead between Nos 1 and 2 holds on the starboard side. A terrific flash lit up the whole ship and then Nos 1 and 2 holds caught fire. No. 1 and No. 2 hatches were blown off and the flames were blazing about 6 feet above the holds. A large column of water was thrown

up and as it landed on the deck it nearly washed me down the staircase.

I sent out a distress message stating that the ship had been hit on the starboard side. As the ship was sinking so rapidly by the head, I thought she would not remain afloat for long and gave orders for the crew to muster on the boat deck and prepare to abandon ship. We carried six lifeboats and at 1820 I ordered five of the boats away, leaving the sixth boat alongside to wait for me. The boats were all lowered successfully and after having thrown all confidential books and papers overboard I abandoned ship in the remaining lifeboat at 1830.

There was a heavy sea and swell and all lifeboats shipped water, however the hand pumps worked perfectly and we had no trouble in keeping the water down. We had all the modern food and equipment in the lifeboats. We pulled away from the ship and lay in the vicinity awaiting a rescue ship.

At 2300 the USN tug *Uncas* closed and picked us up. I told the Captain of the tug that there were five boats in the vicinity, he informed another tug appointed for rescue work – the USS *Pecassus* [sic.] – and together we searched for the five boats. At 2315 the survivors from two of the boats were taken on board the *Uncas* while the remaining three boats were picked up by the *Pecassus*. I then asked the commander of the *Uncas* to close the *Jeypore* which was still afloat although burning fiercely. I found that her foredeck was at water level and her propeller boss just coming out of the water. I contemplated boarding again with a possible view to towing the vessel stern first but as U-boats were still attacking the convoy the *Uncas* was ordered to continue with his rescue work. I watched the *Jeypore* until 2330 and saw a series of bursts of flame come from her, then suddenly die down leaving a blur of smoke. It is then that I consider SS *Jeypore* up-ended and sank.

Chaplain Armstrong aboard the *Restigouche* witnessed the *Jeypore*'s end:

... there was a loud crash and the ship carrying the Convoy Commodore turned left out of the convoy and passed close astern of us as flames roared high in the air and the crew began abandoning ship, jumping from the bridge into the rough icy seas. Some survivors were picked up by a small Navy tug. One of them was

Vice-Admiral E.C. Watson, Royal Navy (ret.), the Convoy Commodore. He was led to the bridge, where Ensign Smith, the tug
captain said, 'What can we do for you, Admiral?'

'A good strong whiskey,' was the reply.

'Sorry sir, but our ships are dry.'

Undaunted, the Admiral produced a small bottle of whiskey
from his parka and passed it among the other survivors. Thinking
the skipper might need a drink before the night was over, he left a
little in the bottle on the ensign's bunk. He later learned it was
thrown over the side.

'Smith was,' the Admiral recalled, 'a zealous young officer, but
still it is extraordinary to send ships to sea in wartime without
"medical" comforts.'

When the furore caused by the torpedoing of the *Jeypore* had died
down, a period of unnatural quiet descended on the convoy. The night
was dark, the wind light and almost playful, and the visibility, aided
by the glow of the Northern Lights, was good enough for ships to
be seen at 5 miles through binoculars. The remaining thirty-one
merchantmen had closed their ranks, seeming almost as though they
were huddled together for mutual protection. Their escorts were doing
their best to provide a screen, but *Celandine* was still astern screening
the rescue tugs, while Piers had taken *Restigouche* ahead to scout for
U-boats.

With the *Jeypore* gone and Commodore Watson aboard one of the
American rescue tugs, the direction of the convoy had been taken over
by Captain Fjørtoft in the Norwegian steamer *Geisha*, a 21-year-old
5,000-tonner which had been nominated as Vice Commodore ship
prior to sailing from New York. Fjørtoft, who had previous experience
as convoy commodore, immediately ordered a series of bold alter-
ations of course, which it was hoped would confuse the U-boats.
Unexpectedly, there was a lull in the attack, and for the next two and a
half hours the only sounds to disturb the silence of the night were the
muffled beat of engines and the slap of waves against hull.

At around 2000, U-132, with Kapitänleutnant Ernst Vogelsang in the
conning tower, approached SC 107 from the south. A Type VIIC out
of the Bremer-Vulkan yard in Bremen, U-132 had enjoyed moderate
success under Vogelsang's command, sinking since her commission
ing in May 1941 eight ships totalling 28,000 tons. She was now on her
fourth war patrol, and had sailed from La Pallice on 6 October.

Mindful of his last brush with the Royal Canadian Navy in these waters, Vogelsang was closing the convoy with extreme caution.

Five months earlier, on his previous patrol in U-132, Ernst Vogelsang had attacked a small convoy in the Gulf of St Lawrence, sinking three ships in quick succession. Elated by his easy kills, he delayed diving, and was lining up on his fourth victim when U-132 was spotted by one of the convoy escorts, the Bangor-class minesweeper HMCS *Drummondville*. The Canadian ship charged at full speed, intending to ram, and Vogelsang was forced to make a hasty crash-dive. He thought he had made his escape, but failed to reckon with the varying layers of density peculiar to the Gulf of St Lawrence. U-132 found herself caught in one of those layers and unable to submerge below 20 metres. *Drummondville* showered her with depth charges, causing major damage to the submarine's ballast pumps. One of her fuel tanks was also holed, leading to the loss of four tons of diesel. At one point, she sank to 180 metres, near to her maximum depth. She was lucky to escape.

U-132 was in no such danger when she moved in on SC 107, for the hard-pressed C-4 escorts were otherwise engaged. Vogelsang's first torpedo, fired at 2015, slammed into the engine room of the Dutch steamer *Hobbema*, leading ship of Column 8.

The 5,507-ton *Hobbema*, originally named *West Lianga*, and built for the US Government near the end of the First World War, was living proof of American 'can do', being completed from keel to launch in just sixty-five days, a world record at the time. She had had a chequered career, having sailed under five different names for six different shipping companies in her long life. In July 1940 she was sold to Sir Robert Ropner of West Hartlepool, and finally transferred to the Netherlands government in exile in May 1942. She was then renamed *Hobbema*, and came under the management of Van Uden Brothers of Rotterdam, being registered in Den Haag. She was commanded by 47-year-old Captain Arie van Duijn, who carried with him a mixed Dutch and British crew of forty-three. The *Hobbema* had already completed one transatlantic round voyage under Dutch registry, and was on the eastbound leg of her second with 7,000 tons of general cargo, which included ammunition.

Exploding in her engine spaces, Vogelsang's torpedo dealt the *Hobbema* a fatal blow. The sea rushed in, her engines stopped, and the ship was plunged into darkness as her generator was overwhelmed. She listed heavily to starboard, and began to founder.

The *Hobbema* carried only two lifeboats, of which the starboard boat was destroyed by the exploding torpedo. The remaining boat on the port side and several life-rafts were launched, but only sixteen survivors were later picked up by the rescue tugs. Captain Duijn and twenty-seven of his crew, including seven British gunners, remain missing, and are believed to have died when the torpedo struck, or were drowned when abandoning ship.

Captain Thomas Muit, on the bridge of the *Empire Lynx* in Column 9, and close on the *Hobbema*'s starboard quarter, was horrified when he saw the holocaust of flame and smoke enveloping the Dutch ship and heard the dull thud of the torpedo striking home. Muit and Captain Duijn of the *Hobbema* were acquainted, their ships having collided in New York's Stapleton Anchorage while the convoy was assembling. Neither ship had received serious damage, but the incident had led to the two captains meeting face to face.

Tom Muit said a silent prayer for the crew of the stricken *Hobbema*, but could offer nothing more tangible, for he had troubles of his own. The 6,379-ton *Empire Lynx*, another relic dating back to the Great War of 1914–18, had been handed down to Britain by the US Shipping Board in 1940, by which time she was suffering problems brought on by her age. Under the management of Glover Brothers of London, she had already made several Atlantic crossings, but now the old tramp's engines were constantly on the verge of breakdown. Heavy in the water with nearly 8,000 tons of cargo, her engineers were having great difficulty in maintaining convoy speed. In fact, much to Captain Muit's dismay, she was barely making 4 knots, and rapidly falling astern of the other ships. Ernst Vogelsang's torpedo had an almost stationary target, and decided the issue. Captain Muit wrote in his report:

> The torpedo struck us in No. 2 hold which immediately flooded, and as there was no bulkhead between Nos 1 and 2 holds, No. 1 also flooded. The ship immediately settled by the bows and sank in four minutes, during which time we managed to get the two after boats away without any difficulty. We also sent out a message to the Commodore ship, fired rockets and put up a red light. All the crew behaved extremely well.

When the *Empire Lynx* was torpedoed, the sea was relatively quiet, with only a slight swell, so although she went down very quickly, there were no casualties amongst the British ship's crew of forty-three.

They spent under an hour in their boats before being picked up by the Dutch steamer *Titus*, which was straggling astern of the convoy after being abandoned and then reboarded. Once on board the *Titus*, Captain Muit was taken to the Master's cabin, where a somewhat shamefaced captain informed him that most of the *Titus*'s crew were still in the lifeboats, having refused to return to the ship after discovering she had not been torpedoed after all. Muit's report continues:

> I boarded the *Titus* about 2100. The Master asked me to his room and explained that his crew were in the boats and that he hadn't sufficient men to take the ship home, there being only a boatswain, two sailors, one engineer and the steward on board; the only officers on board were the Master, 3rd Officer and a passenger acting as 2nd Mate, so it was decided that my crew should take over.

By this time the convoy was some miles ahead, and rather than attempt to catch up, and then perhaps run into a shoal of torpedoes, it was decided that the *Titus* should make a run for it on her own. She eventually reached Liverpool unscathed on 10 November. She was dry-docked on arrival, and a thorough examination of her hull revealed no damage, other than a small dent on the port side.

This was a satisfactory end to an unpleasant incident, but in retrospect it seems unfair to condemn the *Titus*'s Dutch crew for deserting their ship under fire. The records show that they had survived the mauling of Convoy SC 42 in September 1941, when the convoy of sixty-eight ships was savaged by a pack of twenty-one U-boats in a horrific running battle lasting over three days. Sixteen ships had been sunk and four others damaged. Since then, they had criss-crossed the Atlantic many times, facing the same outrageous odds. When the torpedoes had exploded around the *Titus* in the melee of SC 107, those men had reached their breaking point.

Captain Willie Putt, commanding the British India Steamship Company's *Hatimura*, was no stranger to the horrors of war, but even he was shaken when he saw the *Empire Lynx* suddenly up-end and sink stern first. She went down so fast that the likelihood of any of her crew surviving seemed remote.

The 6,690-ton *Hatimura*, a close relative of the Convoy Commodore's ship *Jeypore*, now lying 2,000 fathoms deep, had only recently resumed her station as second ship of Column 7 after dropping astern for emergency repairs.

On the afternoon of 2 November, during all the mayhem caused by the sinking of the *Parthenon*, one of the Canadian corvettes, most probably the *Arvida*, had dropped depth charges within 200 feet of the *Hatimura*'s stern with startling effect. The multiple explosion had lifted the British ship bodily, and shook her so severely that her main feed pipe was fractured. Her engine room began to flood, and Putt had little choice but to drop out of the convoy to make repairs. Darkness had fallen by the time she caught up with the other ships again. Then, on the following morning, she had another narrow escape. Captain Putt described the incident:

> On the morning of 3rd November, just before 1100, I saw a torpedo approaching from the starboard side, but was able to evade it by putting the helm hard to port, and the torpedo just cleared my bow. Three more torpedoes were fired directly after, two of which passed my bow a good bit further ahead, and one struck a tanker, No. 73 in the convoy, which sank at 1100. We could see the tracks of all these four torpedoes which ran through the water just breaking the surface, making a high-pitched whistling noise.

Built in Sunderland in 1918, and acquired by British India a year later, the *Hatimura* carried a crew of eighty; British officers and Lascar ratings. She had traded almost exclusively in the East, and far from the perils of war. This was her first foray into the North Atlantic battle-field, and she had come unarmed. This weakness had been rectified while she was loading in New York, where she was fitted with a 4.7-inch anti-submarine gun, four 20mm Oerlikons, and an array of light machine guns. With the guns had come a crew of ten DEMS gunners. It was hoped that this armament would protect the *Hatimura* from the bad fortune that had dogged her in the past.

In her long career the *Hatimura* had proved to be accident prone, or as some would have it, just plain jinxed. Her first mishap had come in 1922, when she collided with Federal Line's *Cumberland* in the Brisbane River; in March 1926 she ran aground in the mouth of the River Weser; in May 1927, homeward bound from Australia with a cargo of bulk grain, she had sprung a leak and come near to founder-ing; then, in February 1929, she had collided with another ship, this time in the Suez Canal.

The *Hatimura*, having survived all these incidents without serious damage, might also be seen as a lucky ship. However it was the

Bridge of Canadian corvette.
(*Canadian Naval Heritage*)

DEMS gunners of SS *Jeypore*. Lascar crew
mutinied. (*History Buffs*)

Douglas Digbys of RCAF North Atlantic Squadron. (*Shearwater Aviation Museum*)

Ilhas Desertas. *Bullmouth*'s raft landed here.

HMS *Veteran*. Lost with all hands. (*Mark Teadham*)

Long-range Liberator of RAF Coastal Command. (*U-boat Aces*)

Lieutenant Commander Desmond Piers on bridge of HMCS *Restigouche*. (*Legion Magazine*)

North Atlantic convoy in heavy weather. (*NOAA's National Weather Service*)

aron Elgin – and all the time the U-boat continued to circle. (*Photoship*)

US troop convoy bound for Casablanca. (*US National Archives*)

RMS *Queen Mary* in wartime grey.

British and US troops on the beach at Algiers.

General Patton's Western Task Force approaches the coast of French Morocco.

Men of the RAF Regiment marching inland from an Algerian beachhead.

US troop convoy under attack by French aircraft off Casablanca, 8 November 1942.

US troops landing on Algerian beach, 8 November 1942.

opinion of many on board that she was tempting fate when in New York she loaded, along with 8,200 tons of general cargo, 200 tons of TNT, 250 tons of gunpowder and 300 tons of incendiary bombs. These were Class 1 explosives, highly volatile, and to be handled with extreme care. Which is exactly what crossed Captain Putt's mind when two torpedoes fired by Ernst Vogelsang in U-132 blasted their way into the *Hatimura's* holds. Miracles do happen, as explained by Putt in his report to the Admiralty:

> All the gunners were on watch, but no-one saw or heard the torpedoes coming. The first torpedo struck in No. 2 hold on the starboard side, and after a period of two minutes the second struck on the starboard side right underneath the bridge. There was not much noise with the first torpedo, but there must have been a very heavy explosion as a column of water was thrown right over the top of the bridge; the side of the ship was blown out for about 30–40 feet, from the forward rigging to the bridge and we could see the cargo floating out. The hatch covers were still in position. The TNT was stored in Nos 1, 2 and 5 holds, in the tween decks, and although the first explosion was in No. 2 hold, luckily for us it did not detonate the TNT above. I noticed a flash with the first torpedo. The second torpedo made a much louder explosion, but less water was thrown up. Another flash was seen with this explosion.

Although much of the bridge structure had collapsed, Captain Putt and his officers went through the well-rehearsed routine of firing distress rockets, while the radio officers sent out an SOS, and as the *Hatimura* appeared to be sinking rapidly, preparations were made for abandoning ship. A moderate sea was running but, unusually for the Atlantic, there was little swell, and five of the six lifeboats were launched without mishap, the sixth having been damaged by the blast of the torpedoes. From then on, things began to go wrong. Captain Putt's report explains:

> I was left on board with the 3rd Officer and Senior Radio Operator, as some of the crew had panicked and cut the 3rd Officer's boat loose. This boat went away with three Lascars, the 2nd Radio Officer (a Dane), and a ... (deleted by Censor), they did not wait for anyone else. ... (deleted by Censor) was completely demoralized, and they seemed to be in a state of absolute terror.

Meanwhile, the *Hatimura* was going down. She first took a heavy list to starboard, gradually came upright again, and then began to sink bodily. When the sea was lapping over the main deck, the three men stepped overboard, and swam away from the ship. Captain Putt's report continues:

> As the 3rd Officer was a very good swimmer, he succeeded in reaching his boat, and picked up the Senior Radio Officer and myself after we had been in the water twenty minutes. The water was extremely cold, the temperature being 32°F. Whilst I was in the lifeboat I saw a gunner, a survivor from another ship, in difficulties in the water; I tried to grip him, but as he was wearing a heavy coat we could not lift him. A raft drifted alongside with three Lascars on it, they succeeded in pulling him some way onto the raft, but at this point we drifted away and I don't know if they were able to rescue him. I tried to get the gunner in my own boat to help me pull this man on board, but I am afraid he was not much use. I believe he may have had a bad experience during a previous convoy, and this might account for his losing his head so badly.

Safe in his lifeboat, Captain Putt watched as his ship lost her battle with the encroaching sea. She went down bow first, and with a dignity suitable to her age. When the water was up to her funnel, Putt turned away, unable to bear the sight of his command in her death throes. She had disappeared when he looked back, spiralling down some 2,000 fathoms, taking her lethal cargo of high explosives with her. All eighty-six survivors of the *Hatimura*'s crew were picked up by the American rescue tugs. Of their conduct Putt later commented:

> But for the few men who panicked, I was very pleased with the orderly manner in which the ship was abandoned, all my crew behaving well. I would like to pay a special tribute to the No. 1 Marconi Operator, a man named Loughton [First Radio Officer Celus Loughlin], who saw the Assistant Purser drop overboard, and tried to rescue him. Although it was a very dark night he dived into the water without a moment's hesitation; unfortunately he was unsuccessful. He eventually swam back to the ship and climbed up the ladder.
>
> I cannot account for Tomkinson, the gunner [Able Seaman John Tomkinson, RN]. I believe he was on the bridge when the explosion occurred, and although [I] sent everyone to lifeboat stations I do not know what happened to him afterwards.

CHAPTER EIGHT

The US Cavalry Arrives

U-442 ventured out into the Atlantic for the first time in September 1942, having sailed from Kiel on her maiden war patrol on the 17th of that month with orders to operate off the Gulf of St Lawrence. In command was 36-year-old Korvettenkapitän Hans-Joachim Hesse, an officer of senior rank, but with little experience in U-boats. Not surprisingly, Hesse was anxious to prove himself at the first opportunity. This came just a week after sailing, when U-442, passing south of the Faroe Islands, ran into Convoy UR 42.

Hesse could not have found an easier target. UR 42, a convoy of nine small vessels bound from Loch Ewe to Iceland with stores for the garrison, was completely unescorted. Hesse submerged and took aim at the nearest ship, which happened to be the 1,744-ton *Empire Bell*, carrying a cargo of coal from the Tyne to Reykjavik. She was the ex-Swedish flag *Belgia*, salvaged and refitted by the Ministry of War Transport after being bombed by a German aircraft in the Thames Estuary. U-442's torpedo put an end to the *Empire Bell*'s short life under the British flag, and she went to the bottom, taking ten of her crew of thirty-six with her. The remaining eight ships of the convoy scattered at full speed, and Hesse was left searching in vain for his next target.

U-442 continued westwards, and subsequently ran into some of the worst weather experienced in the North Atlantic for more than a decade. Hurricane force winds, mountainous seas, accompanied by fierce rain and hail squalls, brought her progress down to a crawl. She was not alone in her ordeal, for Dönitz had called in a total of twenty-one U-boats to form Group *Panther*. One of those joining the group was U-620, commanded by Heinz Stein. He reported:

Forced under water by the very high swell with the result that the bridge watch has practically drowned and received minor injuries ... The seaman portion of the crew is starting to suffer injuries. All except five men have slight injuries. The other bridge watch keepers have been heavily taxed as I remained on the surface even in the heaviest weather and sought to establish contact. There are now sufficient men for only 2 watches.

When finally in place, Group *Panther*'s patrol line straddled the Black Pit in a north-south direction, forming a 400-mile-long net across the convoy routes. U-442, which had sustained minor damage and one man seriously injured in the atrocious weather encountered, was part of that net. Soon after she was in position, U-258 reported sighting the westbound convoy ON 136, and Dönitz detached eight boats to form Group *Leopard*, which he then sent in pursuit of this convoy. U-442 was one of those chosen for *Leopard*.

ON 136, comprising fifty-three merchantmen bound from Liverpool to New York, had a strong Canadian escort, but the wind was force 10 at the time, with heavy rain, and neither U-boats nor escorts were able to operate with any great effect. Only one ship was sunk before the U-boats called off the attack, this after losing U-597 to a Liberator sent out from Iceland. Hans-Joachim Hesse in U-442 failed to find an opportunity to fire his torpedoes.

The eight *Leopard* boats then went on to take part in an attack on the eastbound convoy SC 104, which was about to enter the Air Gap. This operation, which involved seventeen U-boats in all, and lasted for four days, was more successful. Eight merchant ships were sunk, one of which, the ex-whale factory ship *Southern Empress*, was carrying ten landing craft for Operation Torch.

The attack on SC 104 ended when the convoy came within range of Allied air patrols on the other side of the Black Pit. The *Leopard* pack was dispersed and U-442, once again, came away empty-handed. She resumed her voyage to the west.

There had been little improvement in the weather, and battling against head winds and seas, U-442's progress was so slow that at times she was almost hove-to. October was giving way to November when she finally reached the waters off Newfoundland. The savaging of Convoy SC 107 by Group *Veilchen* was then in full swing.

When, at about 2100 on 3 November, Hesse made contact with the beleaguered convoy, he ran into what might be best described as a hornets' nest disturbed. U-132 had just caused havoc by torpedoing, one after another, the *Hobbema*, the *Empire Lynx* and the *Hatimura*, and the C-4 escorts were thoroughly aroused. Lieutenant Commander Piers had ordered Operation Raspberry, and the night sky was aflame with brilliant displays of starshell and snowflakes. Even the Northern Lights seemed to be shimmering with a new intensity.

Unable to penetrate the escort screen, Hesse dropped back, intent on shadowing the convoy until the furore had died down. And so it was that he came upon the abandoned *Hatimura*, on fire and drifting aimlessly in the wake of SC 107. Hesse was unaware that U-132 was close by and manoeuvring to deliver the *coup de grâce* to the British ship and so draw a line under a highly successful night's work. With no escorts in sight, Ernst Vogelsang had taken U-132 to within a few hundred feet of his target, and as he did so Hesse gave vent to all the frustrations of the past weeks by emptying U-442's bow tubes at the crippled steamer. At least one of his torpedoes went home in the *Hatimura*'s hull.

U-442's torpedo, a mere 750lbs of amatol, acted as a detonator to the 750 tons of high explosives stowed in the *Hatimura*'s tween decks, which had hitherto been completely inert. The massive explosion that followed literally vaporized the stricken ship, and sent a tremendous shock wave scything through the convoy. The Senior Officer Escort, Lieutenant Commander Piers in *Restigouche*, wrote in his report:

> A terrific underwater explosion occurred: it seemed as if the ship had been hit or near-missed. Indeed, the rating employed recording the narrative at the plot wrote, 'Ship hit', and commenced to inflate his lifebelt! All escorts reported this explosion by R/T as having occurred very near themselves. It is believed to have been the bursting boilers of the *Empire Lynx* which was seen to sink just previously.

Captain Willie Putt, who was by then aboard the rescue tug *Pessacus*, said, 'We thought at first that she had been torpedoed, but it later occurred to me that it must have been my old ship exploding under the water, in about 2,000 fathoms, approximately 1½ hours after she was torpedoed.'

It has since been accepted that the *Hatimura*'s cargo was responsible for the blast, but it is still uncertain whether she was underwater or still on the surface when she blew up; but there was no argument about the force of the explosion. Every ship in the convoy was severely shaken, and in some cases crews began to abandon ship in the belief that they had been torpedoed. The shock wave was so severe that it stopped the engine of the rescue tug *Uncas*, which was then 6 miles astern of the convoy searching for survivors, and several U-boats submerged at a depth of 200 feet reported being thrown about. It is claimed that the explosion of the *Hatimura* was the largest on record prior to the first atomic bomb tests in the Nevada Desert in 1945.

Not least affected was the gallant little rescue ship *Stockport*. She had just rejoined the convoy after picking up more men from the water when she ran into the full force of the cataclysmic explosion. At first it was thought that she had been torpedoed, and some of the survivors on board rushed the boat deck and attempted to lower the boats. Captain Fea was forced to take swift action to subdue the panic. A subsequent examination showed that the shock wave had buckled the *Stockport*'s main deck plating on the starboard side, and both her forepeak tank and No. 1 hold had developed leaks. Otherwise, the ship was in no danger.

Coincident with the destruction of the *Hatimura*, U-132 and her entire crew of forty-seven also disappeared, never to be seen again, and it was concluded that in his determination to finish off his victim Ernst Vogelsang approached too close to the burning ship. When U-442's torpedo struck home and the *Hatimura* erupted, U-132 was hit by flying debris, her pressure hull was pierced, and she foundered, taking her trapped crew with her. There were no survivors, so the exact truth will never be known.

The spectacular exit of the *Hatimura* signalled the end of hostilities for the night. The U-boats withdrew, obviously just as shaken and puzzled as their opponents by the massive explosion. The remainder of the night passed in an uneasy peace, with every ship in the convoy remaining on full alert, fearing a resumption of the attack that might come at any moment. Never was the coming of daylight so eagerly awaited.

Wednesday, 4 November, dawned fine and clear, with a fresh westerly breeze, broken cloud, and excellent visibility all round. Were it not for the mind-numbing cold, it could almost have been an early spring day in the Channel. The weather matched the rising confidence in the convoy. Another twelve hours steaming and the ships would leave the frightening emptiness of the Black Pit and come within range of the big four-engined RAF Liberators based on Iceland. And even before that, by nightfall possibly, it was predicted that the US Navy would reinforce the convoy escort force. The destroyers *Leary* and *Schenck* and the Coastguard cutter *Ingham* had already left Reykjavik and were steaming west at full speed.

Hopes of an early deliverance for the battered convoy were running high, but first Lieutenant Commander Piers had a decision to make. The *Stockport* and the two tugs *Pessacus* and *Uncas* had between them a total of 590 survivors on board, some of them injured, and all three were running short of food and water. It was time for them to run for

Reykjavik with all speed, but they could not go unescorted. Reluctantly, Piers ordered the corvettes *Arvida* and *Celandine*, both of which were low on fuel, to accompany them.

Sunset came and went and the short twilight turned to darkness, but there was no sign of the US Navy ships. *Restigouche* had contacted them by R/T, and was trying to home them in by HF/DF, but they seemed unable to find the convoy. That left the twenty-three remaining ships of SC 107 to face the horrors of the night with five escorts, *Restigouche*, *Vanessa*, *Algoma*, *Amherst* and *Moosejaw*, watching over them. The moon would not rise until the very early hours of the 5th, but with the Northern Lights flaring brightly to starboard, the night visibility was good. HF/DF bearings and signals from the Admiralty indicated that the U-boats were gathering in force to make one last assault on the convoy, which it was assumed would come from the south, as before.

On the far side of the convoy, leading the port outside column, those on the bridge of the 4,640-ton *Daleby* considered their ship to be relatively safe. The *Daleby*, one of Sir Robert Ropner's of West Hartlepool, labouring under 7,500 tons of bulk grain and 1,000 tons of Army vehicle spares, was just able to comfortably maintain convoy speed. Captain John Elsdon was aware of his ship's vulnerability, but in tune with the others, he expected any attack to come from the other side of the convoy. Nevertheless, he was not completely at ease, and he had good cause to be so.

Elsdon had already lost two ships to the U-boats. The first had been the 5,219-ton *Clearton*, carrying a full cargo of grain from South America to Manchester in Convoy SL 36. In July 1940, she was 150 miles due west of Ushant, and within short reach of the safety of British waters, when she was torpedoed by U-102. The *Clearton* had not sunk at once, but was limping along behind the convoy when U-102 struck again. This time there was no saving her, and she sank with the loss of nine of her crew. Twelve months later, Elsdon was in command of the 7,005-ton *Empire Dew*, westbound across the Atlantic in ballast, and sailing alone. She was torpedoed in mid-ocean by U-48 and went down in a matter of minutes. John Elsdon survived to sail again, but twenty-three of his crew of forty-one were lost. On that November night with SC 107, the thought was never far from his mind that the third time might be unlucky for him.

As Captain Elsdon anxiously scanned the horizon with his binoculars, Dietrich Lohmann in U-89, who had twenty-four hours earlier sunk the *Jeypore*, and caused the crew of the *Titus* to abandon ship in a panic, was about to confound the prophets by attacking from the port, or northern, side of SC 107, which was largely undefended. At 1940 convoy time, precisely twenty-two hours and twenty-two minutes after U-442 had delivered that disastrous *coup de grâce* to the *Hatimura*, Dietrich Lohmann fired a spread of four torpedoes in the direction of the *Daleby*, one of which hit the target. Captain Elsdon wrote in his report:

> No-one saw the track of the torpedo, which struck in No. 4 hold on the port side. There was a flash, and a small amount of water was thrown up a little higher than the main deck, but the explosion was not as loud as I would have expected. The main deck was set up, but not torn, the hatches from Nos 4 and 5 holds were blown into the air. The engine room bulkhead collapsed. I stopped the engines as the ship seemed to be sinking rapidly.

Elsdon gave the order to abandon ship, and all four lifeboats were cleared for lowering. As this was being done, the *Daleby* gave a violent lurch and a loud rending noise was heard, giving the impression that she was about to go down with a rush. Confusion reigned, the boats were dropped to the water in a hurry, and then, contrary to Elsdon's orders, cut adrift. As a result, after the boats had cleared the ship it was discovered that nine men had been left on board. Those who got away in the lifeboats, which included Captain Elsdon, were soon picked up by the Icelandic steamer *Bruarfoss*. When Elsdon was made aware that men had been left on the sinking ship, he called for volunteers, of which there was no shortage. Choosing six men, Elsdon reboarded his lifeboat and rowed back to the *Daleby*. Prevented from going alongside by the heavy swell, Elsdon called to those still aboard the ship to jump overboard and they would be picked up. His report reads:

> Four of them jumped into the water and as they were wearing their life jackets fitted with red lights we were able to pick them up immediately. The other five refused to jump and said they would sit on a raft on the poop until the ship sank, when they would float off.
>
> At 2310 the ship sank suddenly by the stern at an angle of 45 degrees. The five men floated off but lost their hold on the raft as they did so. A corvette eventually picked up three of them, and

my boat picked up the other two, the red lights on their life jackets helping us to see them.

The rest of the night passed without incident, but the expected reinforcements from Iceland failed to arrive. The three American ships were in touch with *Restigouche* by R/T, but they were unable to locate the convoy in the dark. It was not until it was full daylight on the 5th that the Coastguard cutter *Ingham* and the destroyers *Leary* and *Schenck* appeared over the horizon. Chaplain Armstrong described their arrival:

> The following morning brought a display of grandeur that I will remember until my dying day, as will many of the survivors who lined the rails of the lumbering merchantmen. Knowing that the convoy crews must be shaken by the four days of slaughter, Commander George McCabe (USCG), the skipper of *Ingham*, took the big cutter up and down the lanes of the convoy 'showing the flag'. Running at 20 knots in the heavy seas, her biggest American ensign and signal flag hoists standing out stiff in the breeze, and her crew at battle stations, the sleek blue and grey camouflaged man-of-war was an inspiring sight. As she passed down the long columns, occasionally burying her bow, tough sailors threw their caps in the air and yelled, and tears ran down bearded and weather-beaten faces. The Americans were here! We were saved! The early western settlers must have felt similar emotions when the cavalry rode over the hill to break up a hostile Indian attack.

An hour after the triumphal arrival of the American ships, the first Liberator of 120 Squadron RAF appeared overhead, and the deliverance was complete. The U-boats made a few half-hearted attempts to use their torpedoes, but the combination of air and sea support for SC 107 was now too great for them. They wisely withdrew, but before they left the area U-89 came face to face with an old adversary.

At around 1020, *Restigouche* received a strong HF/DF signal and requested the Liberator to investigate. This it did, and within minutes had sighted a U-boat on the surface 14 miles astern of the convoy. The U-boat in question was Dietrich Lohmann's U-89, and the Liberator H/120 of 120 Squadron RAF, piloted by Squadron Leader Terry Bulloch. Although they were not aware of it at the time, Lohmann and Bulloch had crossed swords some nine months earlier, when U-89 was crossing the Bay of Biscay homeward bound. On that occasion the

U-boat had escaped an untimely end by depth charging when Bulloch, then flying Liberator F/120, had surprised her on the surface. This second meeting was almost a carbon copy of the first, with a stick of depth bombs exploding around U-89 as she crash-dived. Bulloch reported: 'The U-boat was entirely enveloped by the depth charge swirl; the stern rose 15 feet in the air at a 60 degree angle.'

Lohmann had once again had a lucky escape, but U-89 was so severely damaged by Bulloch's depth charges that it was only with great difficulty that she finally reached sanctuary in the Biscay port of Brest.

That night was peaceful, the first for over a week, and with the added protection of the three US Navy escorts and constant air cover during daylight, the convoy reached British waters without further loss, arriving in Liverpool on 10 November. So ended a disastrous Atlantic crossing. Fifteen ships totalling 87,818 gross tons were lost, and they took to the bottom with them 96,800 tons of cargo:

31,400 tons of general cargo.
11,800 tons of steel.
 9,000 tons of fuel oil.
 8,500 tons of grain.
 8,000 tons of tanks.
 7,500 tons of military transport.
 7,400 tons of zinc concentrate.
 6,200 tons of explosives.
 6,000 tons of ammunition.

With those ships went 150 irreplaceable Allied seamen. Had the North Atlantic not been showing an unusually kindly face, the loss of men would have been far greater.

The German version told a different story. An entry in the Naval Staff War Diary read:

Before the air escorts arrived on 5th November most of our boats had broken off the engagement due to lack of fuel or torpedoes. By the morning of 6th November they had reported 23 ships, aggregating 136,000 tons sunk, and one destroyer and one corvette torpedoed.

The German claim may have been grossly inflated, but it cannot be denied that the rout of Convoy SC 107 constituted a major defeat for the Allies in the continuing battle for supremacy of the North Atlantic convoy routes.

Captain Thomas Fea, master of the rescue ship *Stockport*, a man who had witnessed all the horrors of a convoy under attack over and over again, was appalled by what he saw: 'Attacks by enemy submarines were incessant ... it seemed to me just a succession of ships being torpedoed and sinking, and a constant stream of survivors coming on board to be cared for. The sights we saw were heartbreaking. Two steamers, names unknown, were blown to pieces before our eyes, and there were no survivors. Rescue work is very slow, even in good conditions, and in many instances I spent many hours cruising to scattered groups of men.'

In spite of the tremendous risks she was taking dawdling in the wake of convoys to clear up the human flotsam left behind by the U-boats, it seemed that the *Stockport* must be invulnerable. Then, on one dark, storm-swept night in February 1943, her luck finally ran out.

The *Stockport*, acting as rescue ship for the westbound convoy ON 166, had fallen well astern of the convoy while picking up survivors, and was alone and steaming at full speed when U-604 found her. The U-boat fired a spread of four torpedoes, which stopped the little cross-Channel ferry in her tracks, and she went down in a matter of minutes, taking Captain Fea, his entire crew of sixty-three, and ninety-one survivors from other ships with her.

In her two years of service as a rescue ship, the *Stockport* sailed with sixteen convoys and saved the lives of 322 men who would otherwise have perished in the cold dark waters of the North Atlantic. She had earned her place in the annals of the Second World War.

How different were the fortunes of SC 107's neighbouring convoy UGF 1, Casablanca-bound 300 miles to the south. With its huge covering force of battleships, aircraft carriers, cruisers and destroyers, in all it constituted a fleet of 102 ships and was spread over several square miles of ocean. Its accompanying smoke pall must have been visible far over the horizon and there would have been a great deal of radio traffic between ships, yet in sixteen days at sea UGF 1 was never molested, or even threatened by the enemy. It was not until after the ships had landed their troops and were at anchor off Casablanca that the U-boats found them.

On the night of 11 November, U-173, a Type IXC under the command of Oberleutnant Hans-Adolf Schweichel, penetrated the defensive screen around the anchorage and fired a spread of four torpedoes at the massed ships. One hit the 9,359-ton troop transport USS *Joseph Hewes* in her forward hold, and she immediately began to go down by the bow. The sea was lapping over her forecastle head by the time an attempt was made to slip anchor, and it was too late. The *Joseph Hewes* foundered at anchor with the loss of over 100 men. U-173's other torpedoes hit the fleet tanker *Winooski* and the destroyer USS *Hambleton*, both of which were damaged, but did not sink.

Twenty-four hours later, U-130, another Type IXC, followed U-173's example, sinking three ex-passenger liner troop carriers, *Edward Routledge*, *Hugh L. Scott* and *Tasker H. Bliss*. Seventy-four crew members were lost from the three ships.

The fifteen ships sunk in the battle for Convoy SC 107 constituted a disaster in itself, and it came as a culmination of a terrible month for the Allies on the North Atlantic convoy routes. In all, sixty-two ships, 399,715 gross tons, fell to the U-boats. Much of this grievous loss was due to the lack of air cover and the inadequacy of the Canadian escort groups, the latter not through any lack of effort by those manning the destroyers and corvettes, but through lack of experience, lack of numbers, and the outdated equipment carried by these ships.

CHAPTER NINE

Freetown Northbound

As SC 107, battle-scarred and sadly depleted in numbers, slowly emerged from the hell of the Atlantic Black Pit and came under the umbrella of the RAF Liberators, so the northbound convoy SL 125, equally battered, reached sanctuary in the Western Approaches. Of the thirty-seven ships that had set out from Freetown three weeks earlier, only twenty-two remained, and of those seven were badly damaged.

Unlike SC 107, which carried war materials, SL 125 was a run-of-the-mill trade convoy of ships bringing cargoes from South America, the Far East, India and West Africa, just as they had done before the war. They sailed mainly under the Red Ensign, with a sprinkling of Norwegian, Swedish, Dutch, Belgian, and a single American. The Glasgow-registered *Corinaldo* carried a full cargo of frozen meat from Buenos Aires, Hopemount Shipping's *Hopecastle* was homeward from India's Malabar Coast with magnesite and ilmenite ores, tea and jute, Blue Funnel Line's *Stentor* was deep with produce from West Africa. A few, like the ex-Danish tanker *Anglo Maersk*, were in ballast, and there were others, notably Aberdeen & Commonwealth's *Esperance Bay*, which was bringing home military personnel and their families from the East.

The voyage had begun full of hope, with the hot sun high over their yardarms as the ships cleared Cape Sierra Leone and formed up in eleven columns abreast. Snapping at their heels like impatient sheep dogs were their escorting warships, under the command of Lieutenant Commander John Rayner, RD RNR, in the Flower-class corvette *Petunia*.

SL 125's core escort, led by *Petunia*, consisted of three other British corvettes, *Cowslip*, *Crocus* and *Woodruff*, their names evocative of a bouquet of sweet-scented flowers, rather than a covey of extremely effective fighting ships. All were well experienced in convoy escort work, in the North Atlantic and elsewhere. *Petunia*, first commissioned in January 1941, had spent an eventful year in the Western Approaches before being transferred to the West African station, and had recently distinguished herself by rescuing a total of 400 survivors from torpedoed ships in a matter of two weeks. The latest of her rescues had occurred only a few days before sailing with SL 125, when she went to the aid of the Blue Funnel steamer *Agapenor*, sunk by U-87 180 miles south of Freetown. Only hours earlier, the *Agapenor* herself had picked up thirty-eight survivors from the *Glendene*, which had sunk in ninety seconds after being torpedoed by U-125. When *Petunia* returned to harbour, she might easily have been mistaken for an inter-island ferry with a full load of deck passengers. Now, with her decks cleared and her ensign flapping in the light breeze, she was back in business as the Senior Officer Escort's ship.

In support of the four corvettes were the armed trawlers *Copinsay* and *Juliet*, the Free French corvette *Commandant Drogou*, the naval tug *Salvonia*, and what was described as a naval supply vessel, HMS *Kelantan*. The trawlers, the French corvette and the tug would detach for other duties when the convoy was clear of the dangerous waters in the vicinity of Freetown, and only *Kelantan* would remain to go north.

In her previous life the 950-ton *Kelantan* had been one of the 'little white fleet' of the Straits Steamship Company of Singapore. She was a coal-fired steamer, flat-bottomed, with a loaded draught of only 5 feet; ideal for the Malaysian coastal trade, but ill-fitted for the broad Atlantic.

Under the command of Lieutenant Jones, the *Kelantan* had been requisitioned by the Admiralty when Singapore fell, fitted with a 4.5-inch in the bows and a brace of 20mm Oerlikons on her bridge, before being sent out to challenge the enemy. After service in the Indian Ocean carrying troops and supplies, she had been ordered to the UK.

Much of the homeward voyage via the Cape had been farcical. After a serious engine fire at sea, the *Kelantan* had limped into the Seychelle Islands for temporary repairs, which then took her as far as Durban. After more repairs in the South African port, she reached Cape Town, where she then spent eleven weeks in dock. When eventually venturing out into the Atlantic, her engine again failed before she was out of sight of the land. There followed another eleven weeks under repair in the Cape, another eleven carefree weeks for her crew, but a poor contribution to the war effort.

HMS *Kelantan* finally reached Freetown in September 1942, where she was assigned to Convoy SL 125 as a rescue ship and general dogs-body. If she were able to stay afloat and under way, her 4.5-inch gun and two 20 mm Oerlikons might prove a useful addition to Lieutenant Commander Rayner's arsenal.

With boiler fires being stoked and the smoke rolling back from a forest of tall funnels, SL 125 presented an impressive sight as the convoy settled onto a westerly course and began to pick up speed. The route it was to follow, principally to avoid patrolling U-boats, would take it out into the Atlantic for 500 miles, before turning north to pass outside the Cape Verde Islands. This diversion would inevitably add several more days to the passage, but the Admiralty appeared to be in no great hurry for this convoy. As with any convoy, SL 125's speed was dictated by the slowest ship, which in this case was P&O's 5,283-ton *Nagpore*, her best speed being 7½ knots. And someone at that same Admiralty, in his great wisdom, had appointed the *Nagpore* as commodore ship.

If not quite a sister to SC 107's commodore ship *Jeypore*, the *Nagpore* was certainly a close relative, and out of the same P&O stable. Both ships were B-class standard war replacements, built on the north-east coast of England in 1920, similar but not identical. The *Nagpore*, under the command of Captain Percy Tonkin, had loaded in East Africa, and was carrying 1,500 tons of copper, topped off by 5,500 tons of general, all destined for Manchester. She had a total complement of ninety-four, which included the convoy commodore Rear Admiral Sir Cecil Reyne KBE, RN and his staff of six, and five DEMS gunners, who maintained and manned the ship's 4-inch anti-submarine gun. The *Nagpore* was the leading ship of Column 7.

Two columns to starboard, and leading Column 9, was SL 125's vice commodore ship, the 6,148-ton Blue Funnel motor vessel *Stentor*, commanded by Captain William Williams, and carrying the vice commodore Captain Richard Garstin CBE, RNR, and his staff of five. Also on board were 125 passengers, mostly service personnel, and including eleven nursing sisters.

The *Stentor*, built in Dundee in 1926 for the Far East cargo and passenger trade, had a long history of mishaps behind her. In May 1933, she was involved in a collision with the Union Castle steamer *Guildford Castle* which resulted in the latter sinking, then, shortly after the outbreak of war in 1939, she had a second collision, this time with British India's *Dilwara*, while in convoy in the Mediterranean. Fortunately this was a beam to beam collision, and both ships were only slightly damaged. In April 1941, the *Stentor* was a victim of 'friendly fire' when she was bombed and machine gunned by a British aircraft while at anchor off Jeddah in the Red Sea. In each incident the Blue Funnel ship escaped with superficial damage, but she was rapidly earning herself a reputation as an accident prone ship.

Just a few hours after the SL 125 had set course to the west, a signal was received from the Admiralty warning that the troopship *Oronsay* had been torpedoed 500 miles to the south-west of Freetown. Fortunately, the 20,043-ton *Oronsay*, an ex-Orient Steam Navigation Company's liner, was returning relatively empty from a trooping voyage and had, in addition to her crew, only fifty RAF personnel and twenty merchant seamen survivors on board. It was reported that she had been torpedoed by the Italian submarine *Archimede* with the loss of only six men, and that 370 survivors were adrift in lifeboats near the intended route of SL 125. The convoy's escorts were not required to take any action, other than to keep a look out for survivors, but the message provided a clear warning that U-boats were active in the area.

Twenty-four hours out of Freetown, SL 125's seemingly strong escort force began to disintegrate. First to go was the Free French corvette *Commandant Drogou*, which was ordered to Trinidad. A day later, the armed trawler HMS *Copinsay* left to return to Freetown, leaving the convoy looking decidedly vulnerable, but fears were allayed on the 19th when the sloop HMS *Bridgewater* joined. Although the *Bridgewater*, part of the 40th Escort Group, was little bigger than Rayner's corvettes, she was commanded by the experienced Commander Nelson Weekes, RN (retired), and would be a considerable asset to the convoy's defence.

In company with HMS *Bridgewater* came the 12,000-ton troopship ex-Messageries Maritimes' *Président Doumer*, the small Norwegian steamer *Belnor*, and the tanker *British Ardour*. The *Président Doumer* was returning to the UK with 360 military personnel on board, while the *British Ardour* was to act as refuelling ship for the convoy's escorts.

As the newcomers settled in, so another ship was about to drop out. The 7,705-ton British tanker *Anglo Maersk*, sailing in ballast for Glasgow, was nearing the end of what had been a voyage cursed by engine failures. The ex-Danish tanker, requisitioned by the Admiralty in 1940, and under the management of Houlder Brothers of London, had been plagued by serious engine problems ever since she completed discharging a cargo of oil in West Africa. Limping from port to port aided by temporary repairs, she had completed her discharge and finally reached Freetown, where her master Captain Karl Valsberg hoped permanent repairs could be effected. This proved to be beyond the capability of local engineers in the port, and it had again been left to the limited resources of the ship's engineers to get her ready for the homeward passage with SL 125. The *Anglo Maersk* had a 7-cylinder diesel engine, which when functioning well gave a speed of 11 knots, and as the convoy was limited by the *Nagpore* to 7½ knots, Valsberg was satisfied that his ship would keep up with the others. And so she did, until darkness fell on 19 October, three days out from Freetown, and 500 miles deep into the Atlantic.

It was the same old problem, which the *Anglo Maersk*'s chief engineer assured Captain Valsberg could be fixed, providing the main engine could be shut down for a few hours. With the Admiralty's warning in mind that U-boats were in the offing, Captain Valsberg was very reluctant to heave to and lie drifting while the engineers worked, but he had no choice. The Commodore was informed, and hoisting two red lights to signal that she was not under command, the *Anglo Maersk* dropped out of the convoy.

Much to Captain Valsberg's delight, the tanker's repairs were completed in less than two hours and, with the rear ships of the convoy still visible on the horizon, she was soon under way again. It was a false start, for within minutes the *Anglo Maersk* was stopped and drifting again. There followed a long, stressful night and a day with the ship lying beam-on to the long Atlantic swell with every creak of her tortured hull, every clang of the hammers wielded by the sweating engine room gang resonating across the water, clear signals to any approaching U-boat that a helpless target awaited their torpedoes.

Darkness had fallen on the 20th when, after twenty-six hours hove-to, the *Anglo Maersk* at last got under way again. By this time, the convoy was almost 200 miles to the north, and there was no possibility of the tanker catching up, even if she could work up to her full service speed of 11 knots, which was most unlikely. Captain Valsberg was obliged to open his sealed orders, which gave him the recommended route for a ship sailing alone to follow. The remainder of the *Anglo Maersk*'s voyage promised to be a challenge.

In the meantime, SL 125 was 350 miles to the south-west of the Cape Verde Islands and moving north at a sedate but resolute 7 knots.

During the day, the lone American freighter *West Kebar* had left the convoy to sail unescorted to Trinidad, where she would join a convoy for New York. The 5,620-ton *West Kebar*, owned by the American-West African Line and under the command of Captain Dwight A. Smith, was carrying 5,600 tons of manganese ore topped off by 950 tons of mahogany logs, all loaded in West African ports. She also had nine passengers on board, including one woman. Naval Operations in Washington, who had planned the *West Kebar*'s route, were of the opinion that the steamer would be quite safe crossing the Atlantic alone. Captain Smith, with the great weight of ore in his lower holds in mind, was less confident. He expressed concern over the 'very grave and dangerous condition the ship would be in if her shell plating was ruptured'. However, he later wrote, 'Life on board had proceeded at an even tenor, with the crew going about their work in good spirits and the passengers spending their time feeling very pleased about the prospect of a fairly early and safe arrival in the United States.'

Midway across the Atlantic, the *West Kebar* received orders to divert to St Thomas in the Virgin Isles, a diversion which delivered her straight into the arms of U-129. They met to the north-east of Barbados on the black, moonless night of 30 October.

U-129, a Type IXC on her sixth war patrol, was commanded by Kapitänleutnant Hans-Ludwig Witte. When the *West Kebar* unexpectedly came into his sights, Witte fired a single torpedo, which struck the American ship on her starboard side amidships, blasting her hull plates open, just as Captain Smith had feared. Her engine room flooded, and the watertight bulkhead between the engine spaces and the forward holds collapsed. The three men on watch below were killed. Both starboard lifeboats were destroyed by the explosion, but the remaining forty-six crew and nine passengers abandoned ship in the remaining lifeboats and a raft. Contrary to Captain Smith's expectations, the ship did not sink like the proverbial stone, but remained afloat for another hour and a half, at which point U-129 put a second torpedo into her. This broke her back, and she finally went down.

SL 125 did not enjoy the added protection of HMS *Bridgewater* for long. On the 21st, just forty-eight hours after she had joined, the sloop was detached to another convoy. She left at a time when she was most needed.

Inevitably, German Intelligence had been listening to and decoding radio traffic concerning the movements of SL 125, and Dönitz had ordered a patrol line to be set up to ambush the convoy as it passed to the west of the Canary Islands. By daylight on the 25th, Group *Streitaxt* (Battleaxe) was in place, and consisted of eight boats, namely U-134 (Rudolf Schendel), U-409 (Hanns-Ferdinand Massmann), U-440 (Hans Geissler), U-509 (Werner Witte), U-510 (Karl Neitzel), U-572 (Heinz Hirsacker), U-604 (Horst Höltring) and U-659 (Hans Stock). The

U-boats were then to the north of the Canary Islands and sweeping slowly south in line abreast, a 230-mile-long net with 30 miles between each boat, which, in good visibility, would allow for sighting smoke, masts or funnels at 15 miles. SL 125 was by this time south of the Canaries and steaming on a course of 020° at 7 knots. The weather was fair, with fine weather cumulus clouds, a gentle NNE'ly breeze, and clear visibility. The convoy was heading straight into the net being cast by Group *Streitaxt*.

On the morning of 25 October, SL 125 was 200 miles west of the island of Gran Canaria when Lieutenant Commander Rayner received a signal from the Admiralty warning that a U-boat transmission reporting the sighting of a convoy off the Canaries had been intercepted. The report had in fact been sent by a newcomer to the Group, Hermann Kottmann in U-203, who had sighted a lone tanker which he presumed was a straggler from the convoy he had been advised to look out for. On receipt of the Admiralty's signal, Rayner sent one of his corvettes back to investigate, with the result that U-203 was depth charged and her diesel engines damaged. She retired from the action to effect repairs.

Kottmann, quite by chance, had intercepted the *Anglo Maersk*, which having solved her engine problems, was hurrying after the convoy at 9½ knots. She was then, although Captain Valsberg was not yet aware of it, just 50 miles astern of SL 125. U-134 took over as shadower, following in the wake of the *Anglo Maersk*, while the other *Streitaxt* boats were called in. First to arrive was Oberleutnant Werner Witte in the Type IXC U-509.

U-509, built at the Deutsche Werft yard in Hamburg, had been commissioned in November 1941 by Karl-Heinz Wolff. Following a working up period in the Baltic, she joined the 10th U-boat Flotilla in July 1942 for active service in the Atlantic. Her first war patrol, with Wolff in command, took her to the Caribbean at a time when easy targets were plentiful. Nevertheless, after nearly three months at sea she returned without having sunk a single ship. Karl-Heinz Wolff had either been very unlucky, or poorly equipped to command a U-boat. Whatever the reason, when Werner Witte took command of U-509 in September 1942, there was a pressing need to make up for lost time.

With all his attention focused on rejoining the convoy at the earliest opportunity, Captain Karl Valsberg was unaware that he was being shadowed by a U-boat. He failed to see U-509's torpedo racing towards his ship.

The *Anglo Maersk* was hit on the port side in her forward cargo hold. Witte's torpedo exploded with a thunderous roar, and a tall column of dirty water and debris shot high in the air and slammed down on the tanker's bridge like a breaking wave. It brought with it a powerful stench of cordite.

By virtue of its heavy construction, with fore and aft framing, side tanks and numerous watertight bulkheads, an oil tanker does not sink easily, even when its hull is breached. In the case of the *Anglo Maersk*, she was hit in one of her least vulnerable spots, the small dry cargo hold sited between the forward collision bulkhead and the watertight bulkhead of No. 1 oil tank. She staggered, righted herself, and carried on at full speed. On her bridge, Captain Valsberg called for a damage report, and when this revealed the ship to be in no real danger of sinking, he ordered two of the empty after cargo tanks to be ballasted to bring the bows up, and then set course for the nearest port, which was Las Palmas, about 180 miles to the east. The Canary Islands were neutral territory, but under international law the tanker would be allowed forty-eight hours to make temporary repairs.

At 1510, as the *Anglo Maersk* was about to alter course for Las Palmas, a flurry of water was seen astern, and a U-boat came to the surface. Men tumbled out onto her casings and ran forward to man her deck gun. It seems certain that this was U-509, with Werner Witte determined to deliver the *coup de grâce* by gunfire, but he was not about to be given the opportunity. The tanker's 4.7-inch gun on the poop was already manned, and without waiting for orders from the bridge, her gunners opened fire on the surfaced submarine. Their first shot fell short, the second was over, and the third burst close alongside the target. The U-boat immediately crash dived, and without waiting for further developments, the *Anglo Maersk* set off to the east at full speed, zigzagging wildly.

There followed a long, nerve-racking night for Valsberg and his men, but dawn came on the 27th and there had been no further attack. Then, at about 0930, the tracks of two torpedoes were seen crossing the tanker's bows, missing by no more than 20 feet. It seemed that her original assailant had returned to the fray. In fact, later reports showed that four U-boats, including U-509, were now in the vicinity of the fleeing ship.

Nothing further happened during the day, and it was assumed that the *Anglo Maersk*'s pursuers had given up and gone away. She continued to zigzag around an easterly course with an estimated time of arrival in Las Palmas being dawn on the 28th. However, unknown to Captain Valsberg, another threat was drawing near.

U-604, a Type VIIC boat under the command of Kapitänleutnant Horst Höltring, had sailed from Brest on the night of 14 October with orders to operate off Madeira. After a mainly uneventful passage south, Höltring received a signal from Lorient instructing him to join Group *Streitaxt*, then assembling to mount an attack on the north-bound SL 125. Höltring had his first sighting of the enemy at 0936, when he came across the damaged *Anglo Maersk*. The relevant entry in his war diary reads:

> 0936 Mastheads in sight. Tanker, bow left target angle 60° bearing 228°T. Manoeuvered ahead. Enemy speed 12 knots.

Captain Valsberg wrote in his report:

> At 0950 I heard two bumps which shook the whole ship, and seemed to have taken place underneath the ship, but nothing occurred and nothing was visible in the water to indicate what had caused these shocks.

It appears that another U-boat must have fired at the tanker and missed, the torpedoes exploding at the end of their run. Entries in Höltring's war diary point towards this:

> 1000 Sighted own boat (U-509?).
> 1020 Dived for submerged attack, because am ahead of the tanker on the general course.

And then at 1224:

> Because the tanker zig zags heavily, the boat does not come close enough. At range 3500 a three-fan with good shooting data. Shot with target angled red and target speed 12 knots. Miss, probably out of range. Tanker appears grey without neutrality markings and flag. On stern 15.2cm cannon and elevated 7.6cm. On the bridge superstructure and bow anti-aircraft machine guns.

Captain Valsberg's report states:

> After seeing these two torpedoes I altered course to starboard to bring the ship parallel to the direction in which the torpedoes were travelling, and proceeded on a mean course of N 70°E, zig-zagging continually and at 1100 three further torpedoes passed

within 15 feet of the ship along the port side. I had seen the track of these torpedoes as they approached and by altering course further to starboard the torpedoes ran parallel to the ship at a speed of about 30 knots.

The weather was now deteriorating, becoming cloudy with heavy rain squalls impeding visibility. Taking advantage of this, Höltring ran away from the *Anglo Maersk*, and when out of her sight, reloaded his bow tubes. Again using the rain to give cover, he succeeded in drawing ahead of the tanker and waited for her to come within range. At 1805, with the *Anglo Maersk* approaching, Höltring submerged to periscope depth, intending to fire a full spread from his bow tubes as soon as he was close enough. Then, at the last moment, when she was only 550 yards off, the *Anglo Maersk* altered onto the next leg of her zigzag pattern, which inadvertently put her on a collision course with the submerged U-boat. In order to avoid being rammed, Höltring was forced to sheer away to starboard, and had to be content with a quick stern shot.

Much to Höltring's surprise, the single torpedo, fired in a hurry, scored a bullseye, striking the *Anglo Maersk* in her No. 9 cargo tank about 100 feet from the bow. Again, this was not a vital spot, but it added to the tanker's damage forward and she settled further by the head. Captain Valsberg attempted to carry on at full speed, but with her bow section rapidly filling with water the *Anglo Maersk* was impossible to steer. Reluctantly, Valsberg rang the engines to stop and began to make preparations to abandon ship.

U-604 had now resurfaced, and Höltring, having established that there were no escorts around, was calmly reviewing the situation from his conning tower. He watched as the tanker's crew lowered their lifeboats. The port boat went away first with Chief Officer Brandt and seventeen men, followed by the starboard boat with Captain Valsberg and the remaining twenty crew. Under Captain Valsberg's direction, the boats pulled half a mile clear of the ship, then lay back on their oars to wait in case there was a possibility of reboarding.

Suspecting that the tanker's crew might try to go back at daylight, Holst Höltring made another attempt to sink her with another torpedo. This exploded under the *Anglo Maersk*'s bridge, but again seemed to have no visible effect. Höltring, mindful of the strong possibility that the tanker had been in radio communication with the convoy, was reluctant to stay in the vicinity much longer in case escorts came racing to her aid. He tried yet another torpedo, and this went home in a vital spot, exploding in the diesel oil tank just forward of the *Anglo Maersk*'s engine room. At long last, she began to sink.

Forced to witness the destruction of his ship from the lifeboat, Captain Karl Valsberg accepted that there was no point in staying any longer. The two boats now set course for Hierro Island, which lay just over 40 miles to the east. The weather held fair throughout the rest of the night, with a light NW'ly wind and slight sea, and both boats landed on Hierro at around 1400 next day. After two days rest, the thirty-seven survivors began their long journey home via Tenerife, Cadiz, and Gibraltar, reaching Greenock on the *Llanstephan Castle* on 19 November.

CHAPTER TEN

Battleaxe Strikes

While the *Anglo Maersk* was making her desperate bid to reach the sanctuary of the Canaries, Lieutenant Commander Rayner suffered yet another loss to his already depleted escort force. During the night, a signal had been received from the Admiralty ordering the troopship *Esperance Bay* to detach and head for Gibraltar at full speed.

The 14,204-ton *Esperance Bay*, owned by the Aberdeen & Commonwealth Line, had once carried passengers and cargo between the United Kingdom and Australasia, and was requisitioned by the Admiralty in 1939 and converted into an armed merchant cruiser. In that role she carried seven 6-inch and two 3-inch guns, and served with the Freetown Escort Force until November 1941. She was then converted into a troopship, most of her guns being removed. She had no troops on board when she sailed from Freetown with SL 125, but carried more than 200 merchant seamen, who had been stranded in the port for many months after losing their ships.

With the *Esperance Bay* went the armed trawler *Juliet* and the tug *Salvonia*. While none of these ships was well suited to submarine warfare, their guns and their mere presence had been a morale booster for SL 125. As this assorted trio broke away from the convoy and worked up to speed, so U-409 reported to Lorient that she had sighted mastheads on the horizon.

U-409, commanded by 25-year-old Oberleutnant Hanns-Ferdinand Massmann, was a Type VIIC built in German-occupied Danzig in 1941, and was on her second war patrol, which had so far proved unfruitful. She had sailed from Brest on 10 October, and joined Group *Streitaxt* off Madeira. By nightfall on the 26th, she had managed to approach within range of SL 125, only to be immediately detected by Rayner's corvettes and driven off with depth charges.

Acting on U-409's sighting report, the other *Streitaxt* boats came racing in. The relevant entry in Dönitz's war diary reads:

> Contact was maintained by U203 who reported convoy in DH4691 at 0947 on course 45°. Some 11–15 steamers were sighted. Following boats came up to convoy: U409 – 1252; U659 – 1414; U509 –

1703. Contact was temporarily lost on account of gusts of rain and bad visibility. Boats were ordered to continue to search on N and NE courses. At 2259 U510 reported flares over convoy in DH5155. U604 managed to re-establish contact by this, but incorrectly omitted to report same. Boat was forced off about 0430. All this time convoy was steering on NE course in DH5131, speed 7 knots. Weather NW 5-6, showers, medium visibility.

Unknown to Lorient, just after midnight U-203 had fired a four-torpedo spread at three ships which were steaming abreast and over-lapping each other, but failed to score a hit. This attack also went unreported by the convoy; presumably Massmann's torpedoes were hidden by the darkness and indifferent visibility.

The weather had, in fact, turned in the convoy's favour, the rain offering it some limited cover, but it was not going to be an easy night. Word was already being passed around the ships that the U-boats were about, and this was confirmed when, after dark, the Commodore ordered a bold alteration of course in an attempt to lose any shadowers. Two hours later, the ships were brought back onto a northerly course, but as they were limited to 7 knots, little could have been achieved by the manoeuvre. Out in the darkness, at least one U-boat was in contact, and poised ready to strike.

When, on the evening of the 26th, U-509 torpedoed the *Anglo Maersk*, the tanker's gunners retaliated with deadly effect, and Werner Witte was forced to dive in a hurry. By the time the U-boat was checked for damage and resurfaced, her victim had zigzagged away at full speed, and was out of sight. Witte never managed to regain contact with the damaged tanker, but twelve hours later, homing in on U-203's radio bearings, he had the main body of the convoy in sight. Coming up on the rear ships, he went to periscope depth and began the painstaking ritual of overtaking and pulling ahead of the convoy. It was dark again by the time U-509 had slipped unseen past the corvette *Woodruff*, guarding the starboard side, and was in position to choose a target.

The first potential victim to take Witte's eye was a large, deep-loaded cargo liner leading Column 8. Comparison with the book of ship's silhouettes indicated that she was probably a British reefer of the South American trade, and loaded to the gunwales with food to fill British bellies. This was a worthy target for U-509's torpedoes.

On the bridge of Blue Star Line's *Pacific Star*, Captain Griffith Evans, fully aware that his ship presented an attractive target to any marauding U-boat, was intently scanning the dark horizon for any sign of danger. His binoculars showed only the shadowy outlines of the other ships, Blue Funnel's *Stentor* to starboard at No. 91, and the Commodore's ship *Nagpore* to port. Beyond that there was only the rain that marred the night.

The 7,951-ton *Pacific Star* was a twin-screw streamer with refrigerated cargo holds launched on the Clyde in 1920 as the *War Jupiter*, an overdue replacement for First World War losses. On completion, she had been bought by the New Zealand Shipping Company for the then not inconsiderable sum of £65,000, and renamed *Otaki*. This was a proud name, her predecessor having distinguished herself in a running fight with the heavily-armed German raider *Möwe* in 1917. In 1934 she had been sold to Clan Line Steamers of Glasgow and renamed *Clan Robertson*. Four years later, she changed hands yet again, bought by J.A. Billmeir's Stanhope Steamship Company, to become the *Stanfleet*. This much-traded vessel finally passed into the hands of Blue Star Line in 1939, named *Pacific Star*, and became one of Lord Vestey's refrigerated meat carriers. Throughout her long life, she had served considerate masters, who had maintained her to the highest standards, and although now 22 years old, she was still capable of 13 knots.

U-509 approached unseen on the *Pacific Star*'s starboard bow. Witte took careful aim, and fired a single torpedo.

Captain Evans had been on the bridge throughout the Commodore's evasive manoeuvre, and at 1930, with the *Pacific Star* back on her northerly course, he was about to go below for a much delayed dinner. His report explains the sequence of events that followed:

> Weather was fine with good visibility but dark, slight sea and swell, wind NE force 2/3, and we were steaming at 7 knots. We had only just returned to the mean course when at 1935 Convoy Time on the 27th October, in position 29° 16' N 20°57' W, we were struck by a torpedo on the starboard side in No. 1 hold. The explosion was not very loud, but there was a bright yellow flash, a column of water was thrown up and a strong smell of cordite. Nothing was seen of the track of the torpedo, nor of the submarine.
>
> The explosion had very little effect on the ship and we were able to carry on as if nothing had happened. I signalled to the Commodore that we had been torpedoed, and the SS *Stentor*, No. 91, made a signal a few seconds later stating she also had been

torpedoed. We both burned a red light and fired 'snowflakes', but before I could get the rockets from the ammunition locker the ship astern of us had fired rockets for us.

I threw the confidential books overboard in the weighted boxes, closed all watertight doors and sounded round. No. 1 hold had been fully loaded with meat, most of the cargo had been blown out, hatch covers and beams were blown away, and the hold was a shambles, open to the sea on both sides. It was difficult to estimate the size of the hole on the starboard side, but the torpedo appeared to have struck level with the second deck down, almost on the water line, and although this hold was 45 feet in width and fully loaded the explosion had torn the plates on both starboard and port sides. The deck was also badly torn on the starboard side.

I ordered the men to stand by the boats, and carried on. I increased as much as possible, but during the night we dropped astern of the convoy. Although the engines were doing revolutions for 10 knots, we could only make five.

The recipient of Werner Witte's second torpedo, 1,000 yards to starboard of the *Pacific Star*, and steaming neck and neck at the head of Column 9, was the 6,148-ton motor vessel *Stentor*. Built in 1926 for Blue Funnel Line's Far East trade, she was an 'engines-aft' ship, designed for the carriage of tobacco leaf and similar bulk cargoes. The demands of war had brought the *Stentor* to West African ports, there to load 6,000 tons of produce, palm kernels, piassava, ground nuts, exotic timbers, and a full tank of palm oil, all grist to Britain's wartime mill. Under the command of 47-year-old Captain William Williams, she carried a total crew of 107 and seven DEMS gunners. She also had on board the convoy's Vice Commodore, Captain Richard Garstin, RNR, his staff of six signallers, and 125 passengers, a mixture of service personnel and civilians returning home on leave from Africa, among them eleven nursing sisters. Rarely had her accommodation been so well filled.

Although ample warning had been given of enemy submarines being in the vicinity of the convoy, aboard the *Stentor*, in true 'Blue Flue' style, life went on as normal. Dinner was a little late, but the talk in the Officers' Saloon was of anything but war. Staff Captain W.B. Blair, the ship's second in command, was at the head of the table:

Whilst I was having dinner about 1915 I heard an explosion, followed almost immediately by a second. I learned later that one of these explosions was a depth charge from HMS *Woodruff* and the other was a torpedo which struck the *Pacific Star*. I knew that an alteration was due to take place at 1930 and when I heard two blasts on the whistle which meant we were altering course I assumed that everything was in order. I got up and went to the main entrance of the saloon towards my cabin and just as I reached the door at 1935 ATS when in position 29.13 N 20.53 W we were struck by a torpedo in No. 2 bulkhead between No. 2 and 3 holds on the starboard side. There was a moderate swell at the time with wind NW force 4, the weather was fine and the visibility good. The degaussing was on and we were proceeding at a speed of 6½ knots on a course N 52° E altering at the time of the attack to N 12° E.

It was a dull muffled explosion and palm oil stowed in No. 2 deep tank immediately caught fire. By the time I got on deck the flames were leaping 200 feet high forward of the bridge, the fire having spread rapidly to the fore part of the bridge. The oil was pouring into the passengers' accommodation.

Palm oil, extracted from the fruit of the West African oil palm and widely used in the manufacture of soap products, has an ignition point of 600°F, and does not burn easily, but when a torpedo explodes in a tank containing several hundred tons of the oil, the results can be spectacular. This was the case with the *Stentor*. Captain Martin Spencer-Hogbin, then Midshipman Spencer-Hogbin of the *Stentor*, takes up the story:

It was dusk at the time and I was on the bridge, a comparatively raw midshipman. I recall the shock of observing the explosion when the *Pacific Star*, on station 81 was torpedoed, upon which Action Stations was immediately sounded and I went to my position in the chartroom where my duty was to assemble the secret code books in readiness to jettison them if and when necessary. Almost at once there was a huge explosion as a torpedo struck *Stentor* in No. 2 hold deep tank, loaded with palm oil, the force of which ignited the oil and engulfed the whole of the bridge with burning oil. Everyone on the exposed part of the bridge perished, including the Master Captain Williams and the Vice Commodore Captain Garstin. It was purely a matter of chance that I escaped the same fate, being in the shelter of the chartroom.

Four of the lifeboats were lowered and the remainder of the passengers and crew had to jump for it. I have no recollection as to how I escaped from the bridge as the accommodation ladders would have been consumed by fire and my only clear memory is of the *Stentor* going down vertically bow-first after about seven minutes, or so it has been recorded.

One of the nursing sisters on board, Joan Hunter-Bates, later remembered: 'Seventy-five to a hundred faces on the main staircase, stoically waiting their turn to ascend to safety or death. There was no pushing or shoving, just the plain, solid courage of ordinary people. To get out onto the deck I had to duck through a doorway of fire, for the bridge was ablaze.'

Staff Captain Blair described the evacuation of the ship in detail:

I saw Captain Williams by No. 3 boat whilst I was on my way to my own boat which was No. 7. I also saw the Vice Commodore being led along the deck by a Major Turner. As I passed the Vice Commodore I heard him say 'I am blind' and I also noticed that Major Turner had both his hands badly burned.

I went to the boat deck and saw No. 5 and 7 boats safely away. I then turned round with the intention of going to the after well deck in order to release the rafts, but before I had time to do so the ship sank bow first, and I found myself in the water. The ship sank in eight minutes at 1943.

No. 1 boat had been destroyed by the explosion and No. 2 boat by the fire. No. 3 boat had been lowered into the water, but the releasing gear had become jammed, and capsized as the ship sank, throwing all its occupants into the sea. No. 4 boat could not be launched as the fire was too near, and it was finally washed inboard by the swell and smashed against the hatch coaming. Nos 5, 6, 7 and 8 boats had been lowered into the water and filled with survivors.

Some distance astern of the convoy the *Pacific Star* was still afloat, but locked in mortal combat with the elements. As the night wore on, the weather was slowly deteriorating, wind and sea rising towards a violent crescendo. The torn hull plates on the stricken ship's starboard side were acting like brakes, and although her engines were giving revolutions for 10 knots, she was barely making way through the water. Despite all this, with his urgently needed cargo of meat in mind,

Captain Griffith Evans was determined to save his ship, and if possible, to rejoin the convoy. Other than ordering all men not required to handle the ship to stand by the boats, he made no concessions to the *Pacific Star*'s predicament.

The weather continued to worsen, reaching a full gale with a high breaking sea by the early hours of the 28th. By this time, although it was bright moonlight, the rear ships of the convoy were no longer visible, and Evans was forced to concede that rejoining was no longer an option, and that his ship was officially a straggler. This gave him the authority to act independently, and he decided to make for Gibraltar, which lay some 900 miles to the north-east. Unfortunately, this meant putting the wind and sea on the port beam. The *Pacific Star* began to roll heavily, and she soon became unmanageable. At around 0330, course was altered for the Canaries 350 miles to the south-east. This put the sea right astern, and the ship began to sheer wildly each time the sea caught her on the quarter. Another lifeboat was lost, smashed by heavy seas breaking inboard. Captain Evans, for the first time, was beginning to lose heart. He later wrote in his report:

All this time the vessel was slowly going down by the head, as No. 2 hold was flooding through the bulkhead and torn deck plating, until on soundings being taken we found No. 2 hold was completely full and No. 3 hold had 23 feet of water in it. By the evening of the 28th the weather was becoming so bad that I considered it unwise to remain on board. We had five boats left. I ordered the three starboard boats away, as this was the lee side, then turned the ship to make a lee for the port boats. One port boat was launched without much trouble, but whilst we were waiting for the Chief and Second Engineers to come up from below the ship slewed round and by the time the last port boat was lowered it was on the weather side, which made it very difficult to get away from the ship. We finally abandoned ship by 1800 on the 28th, having shut off the engines, but leaving the pumps going as the vessel was going down steadily by the head all the time. I did not attempt to abandon ship in a hurry as it was a very dark night, the weather was bad and I had ninety-seven men to get away safely.

The other drama being played out on the wake of SL 125 was moving at a faster pace. The *Stentor* had gone, her burning cargo quenched beneath the waves, and those who had survived the sinking were fighting for their lives. Staff Captain Blair takes up the story:

> I swam to a raft which was drifting about and managed to scramble on to it. I hailed No. 5 boat, which was a motor boat, and told them not to waste their petrol as I was not sure if the Escort vessels would soon return to pick us up. At 2240 the corvette HMS *Woodruff* returned and picked up the survivors from No. 6 and 8 boats. We were only a few yards away from the corvette on our raft, but the Commanding Officer called out that he was sorry but he had to leave us then, but would return to rescue us.
>
> The corvette cast the two empty boats adrift and went off at full speed. The motor boat then towed my raft to one of the empty boats which the corvette had cast adrift and we got into it, together with some of the men from the motor boat which was overcrowded.

Martin Spencer-Hogbin added to Blair's recollections:

> *Woodruff* arrived after about two hours and picked up some survivors which in itself was a risky business considering the inadequacy of the escort protection of the convoy, but quickly left as her commander Lt. Cdr. Gray reported a U-boat contact, but returned later to pick up the remaining survivors, a remarkable achievement considering the adverse conditions. Most of those rescued were suffering from the effects of oil covering the surrounding sea and from a varying degree of burns, all of whom were taken care of by the crew of the *Woodruff* in what were very confined conditions as there was an increase of 200 in their complement. I have an enduring memory of gentian violet to remind me of the care taken by the personnel of *Woodruff*.

HMS *Woodruff* returned to pick up the remaining survivors shortly after midnight, and it only then became clear that there had been a misunderstanding, leading to the men in the boats being abandoned. When the corvette first arrived on the scene, the *Stentor*'s motor lifeboat was in the vicinity searching for men in the water, and the sound of its engine had been mistaken for that of a U-boat on the surface. William Bromage, serving aboard *Woodruff*, later said, 'The sea was aflame. We picked up a lot of badly burned men. We used mattresses to carry them on board, though when the mattresses folded as they were lifted the men were in agony.'

Many years later, First Radio Officer R. Borrer wrote of his experiences on that night:

I had been relieved from watch to take dinner. As I returned to the wireless room about 7.30pm Second Radio Officer A.N. Evetts took a telephone message from the bridge asking for someone to investigate excessive interference on the radiotelephone.

I asked Mr Evetts to stay on watch while I went to the bridge but then one of the vice commodore's signals staff, who happened to be in the wireless room said he was going to the bridge anyway and would look into the trouble. I then took over the radio watch and Mr. Evetts left the wireless room. Very shortly afterwards the ship was hit by a torpedo and I proceeded to send the appropriate message to the commodore ship and received an acknowledgement. In the meantime Mr Evetts had returned to the wireless room and said the ship was being abandoned.

No more than three or four minutes had elapsed since the explosion when we both left the wireless room which was situated in the port alleyway of the accommodation on the centrecastle deck, abreast the engine room. Stepping from the alleyway to the centrecastle deck, I could see immediately that the ship was doomed. She had a marked list to starboard and had settled so far by the head that the sea was already lapping the centrecastle deck at the after end of the bridge house. The whole of the bridge structure and Nos 1 and 2 lifeboats on the captain's deck were ablaze. Topping this awesome picture, on the monkey island, surrounded and illuminated by the flames, were the third and fourth mates (Mr C.R. Hearne and Mr G.D. Lewis) busily throwing overboard live ammunition from the Oerlikon gun locker, regardless of the imminent fate of the ship.

Yeoman of Signals Geoffrey Clarke, who had been in the *Stentor*'s wireless room shortly before the torpedo struck, takes up the story:

I had gone up on the bridge. It was dark, between seven and half past in the evening. I hadn't been there very long and there was a sort of thump. Contrary to what one might think, there wasn't an almighty explosion and a great big fount of sparks and things. There was just a thump as if we had bumped into something and the effect wasn't immediate. It seemed to be a short while afterwards before eventually the forward hatch seemed to erupt, because the ship was not a tanker but she simply had a deep tank in the No. 2 hold which was just forward of the bridge.

This hold was full of palm oil which we had been told was almost non-inflammable, but it turned out not to be the case because it simply erupted into a huge fountain that shot straight up into the air and fanned out when it got high in the air. It was on fire when it came back down, so it was raining fire on everything and raining an oily fire. My immediate job was two-fold. One of them was to sound off on the ship's siren a succession of S's which was the signal to let everyone know that we had been attacked by a submarine and torpedoed. That was the first thing that I had to do, so I did that, and of course in order to do that I had to go out into the open and pull on the lanyard which operated the thing and all the while it's raining fire.

My next job was to get hold of the confidential books. Those were all the code books which were kept in a bag which was zipped up and weighted with lead so that this could be heaved over the side to make sure the enemy didn't get hold of them: that was my responsibility. Now that bag was kept in the charthouse which was just behind the wheel-house. I was on the port side of the bridge, the torpedo had struck on the starboard side, the other side, and the wind was blowing from the starboard side to the port side.

I opened the door of the chartroom because I knew that the confidential books were in their bag just inside the door on the floor. I went to get them, stepped inside the chartroom door to pick them up, and somebody on the other side of the bridge opened the chartroom door on the other side.

Because the wind was blowing and because everything was blazing, a sheet of flame just shot straight through the chartroom at me just as I was bending down to get hold of the confidential books, and I couldn't get hold of them so I just had to get out.

When I came out of the wheelhouse I sort of had a look at myself and saw that I was in a bit of a mess. I was wearing a short-sleeved shirt and my arms had been covered pretty well with burning oil. It's fairly thick and the skin on my forearms was hanging down in strips, and there were puddles of this oil on the deck. I was wearing gym shoes and the ship was listing and going down a bit and I had difficulty in finding my feet and I kept falling down in these puddles of blazing oil, so I was pretty uncomfortable ... In the end I persuaded myself that the only thing I could do was to jump in, which I did ... There were people in the water, people screaming for help, and the horror of the thing was the fact that we couldn't help them ...

First Radio Officer Borrer resumes the account of what had become a terrible nightmare:

It had not been possible to launch the port boat from the centre-castle deck. The starboard boat had been swung out and, although it had not been lowered, it was waterborne due to the combined effect of the list and the ship settling by the head. This lifeboat was crammed with people, mostly passengers, but it seemed that nobody was doing anything to activate the patent releasing gear.

It was with the intention of releasing this boat from the falls that I made my way diagonally across the centrecastle deck, passing on the way a group of people clustered on the deck just forward of the mainmast. These comprised the master, Capt. W Williams, the mate, Mr A Pope, the surgeon, Dr W. Chisholm, the vice com-modore and some others.

I reached the ship's side by the boat which was being bumped to and fro against the ship by the swell, so I jumped into the water just astern of the boat and pulled myself to its outboard side by the grablines. Just as I was about to climb into the after end of the boat to release the falls the ship upended as though on an axis; the stern rose high in the air and I could see the funnel horizontal against the darkening sky. The ship seemed to hang in this posi-tion for a few seconds before starting to slide beneath the sea.

I was pawing on the ship's side as she was sinking when something caught in the shoulder of my lifejacket, dragging me under. It seemed that my time had come but, surprisingly, in no time I found myself on the surface again. By this time the ship had gone and I was surrounded by other survivors, all looking for something to hang on to in the palm oil laden water.

All this happened so quickly that the ships which had been in line astern of the *Stentor* in the convoy were still passing us in the water at the spot where she had been sunk. I joined a group hold-ing on to a Carley float but this was just about submerged and after a short while Mr. Evetts and myself found and took hold of the wreck buoy. This was a 40-gallon drum with the ship's name painted on its side and a long length of wire spot-welded length-wise around the drum, the other end being secured to the ship's structure. The idea was that if the ship sank in shallow water the drum would float to the surface and indicate her position.

We manoeuvred a wooden hatchboard parallel with the drum so that we could lie across the hatchboard and hang onto the strop around the drum. In this position we were reasonably comfortable and buoyant.

Borrer and Evetts were eventually picked up by one of the *Stentor*'s lifeboats and put aboard HMS *Woodruff*. Borrer commented, 'Clam-bering up the scramble net which was hanging down the side of the corvette, I tumbled onto a deck which was already strewn with sur-vivors. Sailors were dispensing tea and tots of rum but I could see people spewing up their first drink so contrived to have a cup of tea first and, having got rid of that, was able to keep down the warming rum. It was then sometime after midnight.'

When the final roll was called for the *Stentor*, it revealed that Captain William Williams, the Convoy Vice Commodore Captain Richard Garstin, nineteen crew members, including the ship's surgeon Dr William Chisholm, one of Commodore Garstin's signal staff and twenty-two passengers, among them four of the Army nursing sisters, had lost their lives. All died bravely, particularly Doctor Chisholm, of which Staff Captain Blair had to say, 'Doctor Chisholm, the ship's doctor, behaved with extreme gallantry. He calmly continued to dress the Commodore's burns, although the ship was sinking rapidly, sending his assistant away to his boat station, whilst he himself was seen taking the Commodore up onto the boat deck. Both Doctor Chisholm and Commodore Garstin are amongst those missing, and there is no doubt that the Doctor's very gallant action cost him his life.'

Meanwhile, some miles astern in the storm-wracked darkness, Cap-tain Evans had succeeded in abandoning the *Pacific Star* without losing a single man. Ninety-seven men in five lifeboats were preparing to wait out the night. Evans wrote in his report:

We lay to all night in the hope of reboarding in daylight, but by next morning, 29th, it was too rough to return, seas were breaking right over the ship forward and aft, and the fore deck was awash. We had sent out an SOS message before leaving, but nothing came along, so three of the boats set sail for the land, leaving two boats, in charge of the 2nd Officer and myself, to stand by. The two boats remained alongside all the 29th, in the hope of help arriving, as I intended to reboard if a ship came along to stand by us, but nothing came, the weather continued bad, and the men began to get a little restive. However, we stayed in the vicinity all that night until daylight on the 30th, by which time the ship was becoming waterlogged. The starboard propeller was completely out of the water, as she had now taken a list to port, and the ship was so low in the water that she was not drifting, whereas the boats were, so I decided to give up all hope of reboarding, and we set sail for the Canary Islands.

Allowing for drift, Captain Evans estimated that the boats were no more than 80 miles from the Canaries, an estimate which proved to be remarkably accurate. All five boats reached land in Santa Cruz Bay on the island of Palma next day, 30 October. Their reception there was a mixed one, as Evans relates:

> The Authorities were definitely not on our side, the majority of the officials, particularly the Military, are strongly Spanish in feeling, certainly not pro-British, whereas the ordinary man in the street is very much on our side. They treated us very well indeed ... I was interrogated by both the Captain of the Port and the Military Commissar. The former asked me to complete a questionaire, containing such questions as: what our naval Escort consisted of; the distance apart of the ships in columns; ports of departure and destination; the position of the ship when torpedoed; nature and amount of cargo; what was my opinion of the Naval aspect of the war, and if I had seen any bomb damage during the war to ports and installations ... The Captain of the Port was quite a decent fellow and did not press for answers, but the same questions were asked verbally by the Military Commissar who had a very German-looking interpreter with him all the time (I have seen this man at the Canaries several times previously). I gave them no information of any use.

Dawn came at last, bringing to a close what had been a harrowing night for Senior Officer Escort, Lieutenant Commander John Rayner. With only four slow and lightly armed corvettes to stand guard over forty relatively helpless merchantmen, he had known from the time the sun went down on the 27th that he would be attempting to achieve the impossible. He was also wrestling with another problem: *Petunia* was very low on fuel, and it was imperative that she went alongside the *British Ardour* to replenish her tanks. And so it happened that when the *Pacific Star* and the *Stentor* were torpedoed, and *Petunia* was most needed, she was several miles astern of the convoy attempting to catch up after oiling. Those escorts that were present during the attack fired starshell hoping to surprise the enemy while he was still on the surface. It was a forlorn hope, for Werner Witte had long since dived and the brilliant display of light served only to add to the vulnerability of the ships they were protecting.

Since first being warned of the likelihood of an attack, Rayner had begged the Admiralty for reinforcements, but his frantic signals had gone unanswered. In fact, there were no reinforcements to send. Operation Torch was under way, with troop convoys crossing the Atlantic from America and others coming south from the Clyde. In all some 650 Allied ships were at sea, packed with troops and their equipment. These must be defended at all costs. To this end, every available escort, British and American, had been called in to prevent Dönitz's U-boats from sabotaging this great endeavour, on which Churchill and Roosevelt were firmly convinced hung the future course of the war. Convoys to Russia via the Arctic route had been suspended, as had those to South America, with the inevitable result that the North Atlantic trade convoys were so thinly defended that some major disasters were bound to happen. It was happening to SL 125, and would happen to SC 107 too.

CHAPTER ELEVEN

An Evening 'Party'

When dawn came on the 28th, SL 125 was roughly 240 miles west-south-west of Madeira, and steering a northerly course at 7 knots. The wind rose with the sun, and it was soon blowing a near-gale from the west, with a rough tumbling sea accompanied by the usual long Atlantic swell. The deep-loaded merchant ships were making heavy weather of it, while their tiny escorts, true to their reputation, were rolling their gunwales under. This was not the weather to be expected in the vicinity of the fabled 'Garden Isle'.

After the furore accompanying the torpedoing of the *Pacific Star* and her immediate neighbour *Stentor* had died down, Lieutenant Commander Rayner, having rejoined the convoy, rearranged his small escort force in a tight ring around the merchantmen. *Petunia* was on the port bow of the convoy, and *Crocus* to starboard, while *Cowslip* and *Woodruff* rode guard on the flanks. Bringing up the rear was the naval supply ship *Kelantan*, but as she was without Asdic or depth charges, she could never be much more than a make-believe warship. It was Rayner's hope that this strange looking craft might act as a deterrent to any U-boat attempting to creep up astern.

For the time being, the U-boats were not in evidence, but HF/DF bearings indicated that they were still in attendance on the convoy, probably keeping their distance until the sun went down again. Their numbers were increased during the course of the day with the arrival of U-103 and U-440. Group *Streitaxt* now consisted of ten boats, enough to completely swamp SL 125's escorts. Not least among them was the Type IXC U-509. Under the command of Werner Witte she was on her way to becoming SL 125's chief executioner, but she had not always been so productive.

On her first war patrol, U-509, commanded by 32-year-old Karl-Heinz Wolff, had sailed in company with U-508 to join in the 'turkey shoot' that was in full swing off America's eastern seaboard. Ordered to try his luck in the Straits of Florida, Wolff decided to enter the Gulf of Mexico by the back door, passing south of Puerto Rico and Cuba and through the Yucatan Channel. For a man of Wolff's experience the logic of this was hard to follow. U-509 was in waters regularly patrolled by planes of the US Air Force, with the result that she was quickly detected, and subjected to a severe depth charging. She limped back though the Yucatan Channel trailing oil, and there was pounced on again by American aircraft. The stress was too much for Wolff, and he reported to Lorient that he was ill and returning to base. U-509 arrived back in Lorient on 12 September 1942, having been nearly eighty days at sea and achieved nothing. It was now up to Werner Witte to show what U-509 was capable of. This he had already begun by first damaging the *Anglo Maersk* and sinking the *Pacific Star* and the *Stentor*.

Emboldened by his victories of the past night, Witte decided to mount a daylight attack from periscope depth. He emptied his bow tubes into the convoy at random, but all four torpedoes missed. Hermann Kottmann, in U-203 followed Witte's lead, but again wasted his torpedoes. Apart from these underwater attacks, unnoticed by the ships of the convoy, Wednesday 28 October passed quietly. At 1430, Commodore Reyne signalled an alteration of course of 40 degrees to starboard with the object of deceiving the U-boats into thinking the convoy was heading for Gibraltar. At 1830, when it was quite dark, the ships returned to their original northerly course.

The diversion was in vain. Certainly, it failed to fool Oberleutnant Witte, despite being a comparative newcomer to the U-boats. Born in Berlin during the First World War, he had joined the *Kriegsmarine* in 1935, when Germany under Adolf Hitler was beginning to flex her military muscles again. He served exclusively in minesweepers before transferring to submarines in September 1941. On completion of his U-boat training he sailed as First Watch Officer with Heinrich Bleichrodt, one of Dönitz's top aces. He had learned well from the Master, as evidenced by this his first war patrol in command. He had crippled the *Anglo Maersk* and sunk the *Pacific Star* and *Stentor* in a matter of just over twenty-four hours, and then launched an audacious daylight attack. Now Witte was back, with his tubes reloaded, and ready to strike again under the cover of darkness. This time, he had SL 125's commodore ship in his sights.

The 22-year-old *Nagpore* in her younger days had been capable of 11½ knots, but after many years in the Far East was now reduced to a shade over 7 knots, and it is hard to reason why she had been chosen to carry the convoy commodore Rear Admiral Cecil Nugent Reyne.

Reyne, aged 61, was a naval officer of great experience. He first went to sea as a midshipman in 1897 in the battleship *Prince George*, thereafter seeing service in South Africa during the Boer War. At the turn of the century, he was in the gunboat *Partridge* on the West African Station, and throughout the First World War was gunnery officer in HMS *Dreadnought*. He reached the rank of Rear Admiral in 1922, and reverted to the Retired List in 1934 at the age of 53. He was called out of retirement when war came again in 1939, and joined a growing band of his contemporaries as a convoy commodore, with the rank of Commodore, RNR. As such, his task was not an easy one, merchant captains being a fiercely independent bunch.

At 1830, Captain Percy Tonkin was called to the bridge of the *Nagpore* by the Second Officer, who was relieving Chief Officer E.J. Spurling while he went below for dinner. A lookout had sighted a U-boat on the surface crossing from port to starboard close ahead of the ship. While Captain Tonkin was searching the horizon with his binoculars, Werner Witte in U-509, hidden in the darkness to starboard, emptied his bow tubes at the massed ranks of shipping. Chief Officer Spurling, who at that point was on his way back up to the bridge, later recorded the sequence of events:

> The torpedo struck on the starboard side amidships. The explosion was not very loud but a large column of water must have been thrown up as the bridge was covered in water when I went up to it. No flash or flame was seen from the explosion. The starboard side of the accommodation was blown in and the starboard wing of the bridge collapsed. No. 1 port lifeboat was badly wrecked and as soon as we tried to lower No. 3 port boat it broke into two pieces. The hatches were blown off No. 3 hold and the saddle bunker abaft the funnel had the hatches blown off. All the ladders to the bridge were blown away but the bridge remained intact except for the starboard wing. The R/T set collapsed and the entrance to the wireless room was blocked by fallen debris. The ship remained on an even keel and did not lift with the explosion.

The *Nagpore* carried a total of seven lifeboats, five of her own in the davits, and two others on the hatch tops acquired when picking up survivors from the Danish motor vessel *Siam II* when she was on her way north from the Cape. The *Siam II*, also bound for Freetown, had been torpedoed by U-506 on 1 October when 330 miles south-west of Monrovia. Her thirty-nine survivors had been landed in Freetown, but her boats had remained with the *Nagpore*.

Despite having a surplus of boats, the evacuation of the *Nagpore* was chaotic. The first boat away contained only one officer, Fourth Engineer J.J. Marshall, and an estimated thirty Lascars. Marshall, young and without any experience in boat work, had no control over the Lascars, who were in a complete panic. With the help of officers on the boat deck, the boat reached the water, but drifted away and was swallowed up in the storm-filled darkness. Next away was the forward starboard boat, rushed by about forty Lascar crew, who lowered the boat without orders and almost wrecked it. It was fortunate that Chief Officer Spurling was able to board by shinning down one of the manropes. He restored some semblance of order, but by this time the boat, having been slammed against the ship's side by the swell, was leaking badly. No other lifeboats got away.

The weather prevailing at the time (it was blowing a full gale), the panicking crew, and the total darkness, all played a part in the shambles of that night. Unfortunately, it was a scene to be repeated in British ships far too often in the war, and many lives were needlessly lost in this way. The root cause in most cases was the lack of practice by merchant ships' crews in boat handling, a situation largely brought about by complacency and a belief in the old adage 'your ship is your best lifeboat'. Fortnightly lifeboat drills, mandatory under the law of the sea, had in all too many ships degenerated into a brief roll call on the boat deck on a Saturday morning, followed by a mad dash to down a couple of beers before lunch. Boats were rarely swung out, and more rarely lowered to the water. It was well known that many shipowners regarded lifeboats as an expensive necessity forced on them by law, and openly discouraged the frivolous use of them. For voyage after voyage a ship's lifeboats would remain firmly in their davits, a practice condoned by masters and officers. When war came and abandoning a sinking ship became an all too frequent reality, an inability to launch lifeboats simply through lack of practice led to many brave men losing their lives needlessly.

At 1910, just ten minutes after she had been torpedoed, the *Nagpore* broke her back; her bow and stern rose majestically in the air, and with her two masts leaning inwards so that their topmasts almost touched, she slid beneath the waves, taking her valuable cargo of copper to the bottom with her. As she went down, one of the *Siam II*'s lifeboats floated off, but only two of the ship's gunners and two Lascars managed to clamber aboard before it drifted away.

Captain Percy Tonkin and First Radio Officer Laurence Gledhill were last seen on the *Nagpore*'s lower bridge, and were presumed to have gone down with her. Commodore Cecil Reyne was knocked unconscious by floating wreckage, but was saved from drowning by Third Officer Horace Waters, who supported him for two hours while waiting for help to come. Many of the others struggling in the water owed their lives to four small buoyant floats that came to the surface after the *Nagpore* went down. Rescue, when it came, was a matter of pure chance. Lieutenant John Holm, commanding the corvette HMS *Crocus*, described the drama of the night in his book *No Place to Linger*, published in 1985:

> Soon after the start of that evening's 'party' the convoy did an emergency turn to port, but due to the bad visibility and to the fact that the *Crocus*'s radar was temporarily out of action, we missed this alteration, made by light signals to avoid helping any U-boat home in on us. We remained in ignorance of the turn until the next morning.
>
> Soon after darkness descended, there was a great deal of commotion inside the convoy with explosions, ships on fire and snowflake rockets being fired as well as tracer bullets from machine guns. We followed our prescribed search pattern but saw no sign of U-boats, and then took a quick look across the stern of the convoy where there was now no escort. Just as we were turning away to resume station, our alert lookouts spotted lights in the water away to port. We turned to investigate and ended up in a mass of wreckage that had once belonged to the good ship *Nagpore*.
>
> There was one boatload of survivors and a grossly overloaded Carley float. It was not an easy job getting them on board and careful manoeuvring was needed to make a lee shelter and to avoid cutting them to pieces with our propeller. The sea was tossing them up above our quarter one minute and away below it the next and we wondered afterwards how they ever managed to scramble aboard. But this many of them did, with the help of our men and our overside scrambling nets and, to the best of my knowledge, without any major injuries.

Battling against a steep breaking sea, *Crocus* rolled and pitched like a demented mule, and it took all of Holm's seamanship skills to hold her close enough for the men in the water to reach the scrambling nets.

It was just as well he had learned his trade well, going to sea in sail as a boy, then tramping the oceans in merchant steamers, before enlisting in the Royal New Zealand Navy in 1940. Two punishing years on the North Atlantic convoy routes had completed his education. Ship handling in heavy weather was second nature to John Holm.

Then, as Holm fought to save the *Nagpore*'s men, *Crocus*'s Asdic operator detected the unmistakeable sound of a torpedo running. Seconds later came the cry from aft, 'Torpedo wake passing starboard quarter!' And while the wind howled, the waves crashed, and his ship strove to emulate a sounding whale, Holm was faced with an awesome decision; should he carry on with the rescue and risk the lives of all on board, or should he go after the U-boat? Hesitating only for a brief moment, he hauled *Crocus* short round, rang for full speed, and charged after the enemy.

Careering from crest to trough, her blunt bows slamming into the angry seas, her decks streaming with foaming green water, *Crocus* went after her erstwhile attacker with the enthusiasm of a dog after a rabbit. But the U-boat had gone deep, with no echoing Asdic ping to point to her whereabouts. Holm dropped two single depth charges, but they were no more than a relief for his frustration. He then reversed course and went back for the *Nagpore*'s survivors.

At the end of a harrowing but on the whole satisfying night's work, *Crocus* had snatched from the waiting arms of the Grim Reaper thirty-four wet, cold and half-drowned men, including Commodore Cecil Reyne and five of his staff. Many years later, John Holm wrote:

> After things had settled down a little, Leading Sick Bay Attendant Ife appeared on the bridge to report on the condition of our survivors. He had the Convoy Commodore among them, he told me, and had taken the liberty of putting him in my bunk, as the Commodore had been plucked from the underside of the Carley float and was unconscious, almost dead, when hauled aboard. In their rush to give him artificial resuscitation before it was too late, they had slit up the back of his clothing with a sharp knife to get it off. It was reported that the Commodore, another ex-Admiral, was now breathing normally and sleeping quietly. One or two of the others had not come through the ordeal quite so well, but mostly they were fit and grateful.

When the final count was made, it was found that Captain Percy Tonkin, First Radio Officer Laurence Gledhill, Second Radio Officer

Jack Dunstan, chief Steward Frederick Passingham and eighteen Indian ratings had lost their lives. Ironically, the lifeboat in charge of Fourth Engineer Marshall made a landfall at Puerto Orotava, on the northern coast of Tenerife fourteen days later. The boat's rudder had been smashed in the chaotic lowering, with the result that her passage to the Canaries, much of it in gale force conditions, had been a supreme test for the young engineer. Marshall kept a log, in which he wrote on the 30th: 'Constant bailing out of water. Did not dare hoist sail as storm terrific.' It is to Marshall's great credit that he maintained order in the boat, forcing the largely disinterested occupants to massage their feet to avoid foot rot, and burning flares when ships were sighted. Several ships passed close, but ignored Marshall's distress signals. The only contact they had was when they came across a German supply tanker, with a U-boat alongside refuelling. The U-boat sent a party across to interrogate the survivors, but the Germans offered no assistance. Marshall carried on his lone voyaging and, when he eventually reached land, of the thirty men it had originally carried, only eighteen were still alive.

Lieutenant Holm's report continued:

As dawn came slowly over the angry sea, we looked anxiously for the convoy ahead. It was nowhere to be seen. Strange, I thought. The convoy should have been there and not far away, as it would have been slowed down by the attacks and resulting confusion, and we were making a good three knots faster. I decided that it was likely that an emergency turn had been made. And it must have been to port, away from *Crocus*, or they would have come over the top of us. Commodore said the turn had been 40 degrees to port.

At this point Holm received a report from the radar room that the set was now working again, and would hopefully lead *Crocus* back to the convoy. A few minutes later, more good news, when a single echo, resembling that of a large ship, was reported ahead. Lieutenant Holm wrote:

Suddenly the radar reported a blip ahead and in ten minutes we were circling a ship that we saw in the beam of our searchlight was the SS *Hopecastle*. Although she seemed perfectly seaworthy, there was no sign of life on board and no response to our hailing. Then came another radar echo close by. This was the *Tasmania*, undamaged and with the entire crew of the *Hopecastle* aboard. *Tasmania*'s Captain told me *Hopecastle* had been hit forward but her Chief Engineer stated that, although damaged, the engine-room was intact and he felt the ship would remain afloat.

It was now midnight, and we had no time for a lame ship with no men aboard. We had to look after the live ones. I asked over the loudhailer if all the *Hopecastle*'s confidential books had been destroyed and, on being assured that they had, we set off again for our neglected station, with *Tasmania* following. Full ahead, and again *Crocus* responded more like a bucking bronco than the lady she could be, as she bashed her way through the heavy seas. She knew that lives and ships could depend on our getting back to the convoy without delay.

Crocus's searchlight had revealed the 5,187-ton motor vessel *Hope-castle*, last seen near the head of SL 125's Column 8. Owned by the Hopemount Shipping Company of Newcastle, and commanded by 49-year-old Captain Dugald McGilp, the *Hopecastle* was one of a new breed of North-East Coast tramps. Although broad in the beam with a huge cargo-carrying capacity, she was a far cry from the tall-funnelled rust buckets of the twenties and early thirties. Built at the Swan Hunter yard in Sunderland in 1937, she was a fine-looking motor vessel, well equipped, with a service speed of 12 knots. In other respects, she was no different to the archetypal British tramp, at the beck and call of the charter market, ready to go anywhere there was cargo on offer, and given to extended voyages.

The *Hopecastle*'s current voyage had begun six months earlier in the Bristol Channel, where she loaded Army stores and ammunition for the Middle East. With the Mediterranean closed to Allied shipping, she took the long route around the Cape of Good Hope, then ran the gauntlet of Japanese submarines in the Indian Ocean to discharge her cargo at Suez. Ballasted, she had crossed to India's west coast, where she filled her holds with 2,500 tons of magnesite and ilmenite ores, topped off by 3,000 tons of tea in chests and bales of jute. She was *full cubic, full deadweight*, every shipowner's dream of perfection. Rounding the Cape again, she had reached Freetown and joined Convoy SL 125 for the final leg of her voyage. It was on that last lap, having covered 23,000 miles, the equivalent of a circumnavigation of the globe, with only 1,500 miles to go to voyage end, that the *Hopecastle* crossed paths with U-509.

When Werner Witte made his attack on SL 125 in the early evening of the 28th, flushed with his success in disposing of the *Anglo Maersk*, the *Pacific Star* and the *Stentor*, he had fired at random; four torpedoes from his bow tubes, followed by one from his stern tubes. There seemed to be no end to U-509's luck, for not only did her torpedoes sink the *Nagpore*, but they also put an end to the *Hopecastle*'s long voyage. Second Officer J.R. Petrie, who was on watch on the bridge of the *Hopecastle* at the time, wrote in a report for the Admiralty:

At 2010 GMT when in position 160' S 60° W (true) from Madeira whilst steering 355° at a speed of 7 knots we were struck by a torpedo. The weather was fine and clear, visibility good, the sea was rough with a heavy swell and wind NW force 6/7. We were struck on the starboard side in the after end of No. 2 hatch just forward of the bridge. I was on watch on the bridge at the time and was temporarily knocked unconscious so were all those who were with me. I cannot remember hearing the explosion or seeing anything. When I eventually came to I found that the starboard jolly boat had been destroyed but that all the other boats were intact. The hatches and beams of Nos 1 and 2 holds had been blown off. The engines were still going ahead and as the ship had settled down forward she was shipping heavy seas over the fore-castle head and fore deck. It was impossible to ascertain the full extent of the damage as it was a very dark night. The PAC Rockets and snowflakes had ignited while we were unconscious and were flying around the bridge, and those from the port side were in the water and burning brightly. I could not hear anything when I first became conscious neither could the Chief Officer. We found the Captain very badly injured, he had lost an eye and the whole of his face was mutilated, the apprentice also had face injuries but not so severe.

With the exception of one Junior Engineer, who had been killed when the torpedo struck, the *Hopecastle*'s entire crew of forty-four were picked up by the Danish crewed, British flag, *Tasmania*, which, at great risk to herself, and strictly against orders, had dropped back to help. Whether or not the *Hopecastle* should have been abandoned is debatable. Her Chief Engineer later stated that although there was damage in her engine room, the machinery was still intact, and that he thought she would stay afloat. However, in view of the fact that Captain McGilp was grievously injured, it may be that there was a lack of leadership in this matter. In any case, the *Hopecastle* was not to last much longer, as U-203 had arrived on the scene.

U-203, a Type VIIC out of the Germania yard at Kiel, was commissioned in February 1941 by Kapitänleutnant Rolf Mützelburg, and for much of her career enjoyed considerable success. In seven patrols with Mützelburg in command, she sank nineteen Allied merchantmen, totalling some 88,000 tons of shipping. Then, on her eighth patrol, she ran into trouble.

Sailing from Brest on 28 August 1942, U-203 made her first dive while crossing the Bay of Biscay, and to Mützelburg's dismay it was discovered that a vital valve in the pressure hull was leaking. Closer examination showed that the valve had been poorly secured, probably sabotaged while the boat was in Brest. Fortunately, U-203's engineers were able effect a repair at sea, and Mützelburg continued with the voyage.

Two weeks out from Brest, on 11 September, U-203 was on station 160 miles south-west of the Azores awaiting orders. The weather was fine and warm, the sea calm, and Mützelburg took advantage of the lull to allow his crew to go swimming. He joined in the fun, diving off the conning tower, but as he dived the boat lurched in the swell, and Mützelburg struck his head on the pressure hull. He was dragged from the water unconscious, but died a few hours later from a fractured skull. He was buried at sea next day. Leutnant Hans Seidel, U-203's First Watch Officer, now took command, and brought the boat back to Brest. She sailed again in early October with Oberleutnant Hermann Kottmann in command.

Hermann Kottmann was on his first voyage in command, and was also new to the U-boats. An ex-gunnery officer of the pocket battleship *Graf Spee*, he had been interned in Montevideo when his ship was scuttled, but escaped to Chile. A Japanese merchantman took him to Japan, and he was repatriated to Germany. After serving in the feared SS for a year, he joined the U-boat arm and took command of U-203 in September 1942. He remained a dedicated Nazi and, as such, he was not popular with his crew.

When, in the small hours of the 29th, Kottmann found the *Hopecastle*, abandoned and drifting aimlessly some 40 miles astern of SL 125, he used a single torpedo to administer the *coup de grâce*. Surprisingly, the British ship, although already listing to starboard and down by the head, stubbornly refused to sink. Having used a full spread of torpedoes earlier in the day with no perceivable gain, Kottmann was unwilling to waste another. The weather was too rough to man the deck gun, so he resorted to the 20mm canon which, after a great expenditure of ammunition, eventually set the *Hopecastle* on fire. Only then, with dawn paling the sky to the east, did the Newcastle tramp sink.

It was later established that Captain Dugald McGilp, Apprentice John Charlton, Junior Engineer Raymond Carr, and DEMS gunners Sergeant Walter Hill, Royal Marines and Lance Bombardier Stanley Radcliffe, Royal Artillery all lost their lives with the *Hopecastle*. The names of the first three are inscribed on a plaque at the Merchant Navy Memorial on London's Tower Hill. The DEMS gunners are remembered elsewhere. Junior Engineer Carr is believed to have died when the first torpedo hit, while it is possible that the others stayed aboard the *Hopecastle* in an attempt to save her.

The convoy was by now in a state of complete chaos, with ships and escorts scattered over a very wide area. The *Nagpore* having gone and Commodore Reyne aboard *Crocus*, Lieutenant Commander Rayner appointed Captain W.A. Haddock, master of the *Empire Cougar*, as convoy commodore. Speed was reduced to 6 knots to allow the stragglers to catch up.

CHAPTER TWELVE

A Rare Gale

When Hermann Kottmann's U-203 finally put an end to the *Hope-castle's* voyaging early on the morning of 29 October, Convoy SL 125 was still faced with at least another five days hard steaming before it came within range of British air cover, or any other form of assistance. There had been some improvement in the weather, in that the sky had cleared and visibility was good, a mixed blessing perhaps, but the wind was still blowing force 6/7 and generating a very rough sea. When daylight came there was little in the way of optimism in the air. Lieutenant Commander Rayner had done well to bring a semblance of order back to the convoy, but nothing could disguise the fact that SL 125 had suffered a severe roughing up at the hands of the *Streitaxt* boats. Five ships had gone, consigned to the bottom of the ocean, or drifting out of sight astern disabled and abandoned by their crews. And as Rayner ran his binoculars over the depleted columns of his convoy, yet another ship was dropping out, signalling that she had an engine breakdown. She was the British motor tanker *Bullmouth.*

The *Bullmouth* was held in special regard by the men of the convoy escorts, as she had for some months past been their fuelling tanker in Freetown harbour. Lieutenant John Holm, commanding HMS *Crocus*, said of her: 'She was always our first stop on arrival back at base and the ship from which we got our ever-welcome mail. We had come to know her officers and company well and I had had many a pink gin with her Captain while catching up on the gossip of the Freetown Escort Force, and telling him the story of our latest venture ...'

All those months lying at anchor in the warm waters of Sierra Leone had resulted in the *Bullmouth's* bottom being thick with barnacles and weed and her engines sorely in need of a major overhaul. Now she was paying the price of so much inactivity. Her engines were still turning out the revolutions, but because of her foul bottom she had been losing speed for some time, and could no longer keep up with the other ships. Soon she would be on her own, and although she had nothing more lethal than water ballast on board, the U-boats were not to know, and the fact that she was a tanker made her a prime target. Much as he would have liked to offer the tanker protection, with only four corvettes to cover a convoy spread out over 9 or 10 miles of ocean Lieutenant Commander Rayner was powerless to help. He had continued to badger the Admiralty for reinforcements, but his pleas were falling on deaf ears, and with good reason. Operation Torch was in full swing.

The first of the British supply convoys for Torch had sailed from the Clyde on 2 October, to be followed on the 22nd by the fast troop convoys. By dawn on the 26th, eight convoys were at sea and making their way south to Gibraltar. They comprised 190 merchant ships and 76 naval escorts, a long procession of ships stretching from the Western Approaches to Cape St Vincent. Additional anti-submarine vessels were patrolling the Bay of Biscay hunting for U-boats in transit that might pose a threat, while in the Denmark Strait, between Greenland and Iceland, heavy units of the Home Fleet were stationed, ready to intervene should any of Admiral Raeder's big ships leave their hiding places in the Norwegian fjords. In the air over the Atlantic, long-range aircraft of RAF Coastal Command gave cover to the convoys, while RAF Bomber Command and aircraft of the 8th US Air Force were pounding the U-boat bases in the French Biscay ports. In the words of Winston Churchill, 'Our great armadas were approaching the scene. We were determined to spare nothing to safeguard their passage.' In effect, at that time only Torch mattered; the routine trade convoys, of which SL 125 was one, were left to fight their own battles with whatever they had to hand.

Ironically, *B-Dienst*, the German intelligence agency, was completely unaware of the Allied intention to invade French North Africa. Its agents in Spain were reporting a massive build-up of shipping at Gibraltar, but this the German Naval Staff believed was in preparation for an attempt to relieve the beleaguered island of Malta. This was confirmed by a statement issued by Berlin later: 'At the beginning of October we noticed increased activity by British Naval forces and shipping at Gibraltar, but although this aroused some suspicion, we believed that it was connected with a major convoy operation for the relief of Malta, and that did not imply a landing in North Africa.' The U-boats were told to get on with their usual business of harassing the trade convoys.

Captain William Anderson, commanding the Donaldson Line steamer *Corinaldo*, was becoming increasingly concerned at the mounting danger threatening his ship. She had been directly astern of the *Pacific Star* when U-509's torpedo blew a hole in her side, and witness to the demise of the *Stentor* shortly afterwards. Twenty-four hours later, Anderson had watched in horror as the Commodore's ship *Nagpore* staggered out of line and began to sink, followed five minutes later by the *Hopecastle*. When the *Hopecastle* went, with her exploding snowflake rockets brilliantly illuminating the scene of carnage, a U-boat was sighted on the surface on the *Corinaldo's* port quarter, and approaching obviously intent on another kill. Anderson had acted quickly. Putting the helm hard to starboard to spoil the U-boat's aim, he ordered his gunners to open fire. The port Hotchkiss on the bridge had responded immediately, a long line of tracer reaching out for the attacker. As the machine gun bullets struck sparks off the U-boat's conning tower, the *Corinaldo's* 4-inch gun opened up, landing shells close alongside the submarine. There was a roar as the enemy's main ballast was flooded, and she disappeared in a welter of foam.

The scene was rapidly beginning to resemble some bizarre coconut shy set in a blacked out fairground in the midst of a howling gale. The half-submerged *Streitaxt* boats were taking turns about to slip through Rayner's totally inadequate defensive screen and fire at random at the mass of helpless merchantmen, withdrawing as soon as their torpedoes had left their tubes.

What remained of the night was relatively quiet, the sated U-boats having withdrawn, presumably to reload. But this was not a signal for relaxation. After her narrow escape, the *Corinaldo's* crew were on full alert. All guns remained fully manned, and not a man dared to move without his life jacket at hand.

And so it remained during the daylight hours on the 29th, tension building all the time. Nerves were at full stretch, and by late afternoon the strain was beginning to take its toll. Appalled by the necessity to maintain the convoy speed of 7 knots, which he considered to be suicidal under the circumstances, Captain Anderson had reached the point where he was seriously thinking of breaking ranks and going it alone at full speed.

The 7,131-ton *Corinaldo*, the product of a front-rank Clyde shipyard, was 21 years old, but she had been well cared for. A ship before her time, she was powered by two steam turbines, which even after so many years in the trade still gave her a speed of 12 knots, and more if pushed. However, in her refrigerated holds she carried 5,000 tons of Argentinian beef, a cargo desperately needed by the food-short households of Britain. No matter how frustrated he might feel, William

Anderson simply could not afford to put his ship in any more peril than she already faced.

Mercifully, the day passed peacefully, with SL 125 finding time to consolidate its ranks, and the U-boats, presumably, unwilling to risk an attack in daylight, even though the convoy was plainly poorly protected. It might even have been a pleasant day, were it not for the rapidly worsening weather. The north-westerly wind had increased to Force 7, and was accompanied by fierce rain squalls. This, and a menacingly heavy swell and rough sea, made life very uncomfortable for the blunt-bowed merchantmen, some of whom were struggling to make headway at all. The weather, possibly due to a large depression moving in from the Atlantic, was completely out of keeping for the area, where the North-East Trades usually dominate throughout the year. The Africa Pilot advises: 'In this region winds are strongest in the summer months (averaging approximately 12–14 knots in July and August) and lightest in October or November when the monthly average is 9–10 knots. Gales (force 8) are rare.'

With the sky heavily overcast, darkness closed in early; a little after 1700. The wind was howling in the rigging, the big seas slamming against the slowly moving hulls, promising a thoroughly miserable night. On the bridge of the *Corinaldo*, Captain Anderson paced up and down impatiently. The convoy's speed was by now down to 4 knots, a mere crawl, and Anderson felt desperately vulnerable. And, as it turned out, he had good cause to worry.

At precisely thirty minutes after eight, two torpedoes slammed into the *Corinaldo*'s port side, one exploding in her No. 1 hold, the other hitting immediately abaft her bridge.

Anderson wrote in his report:

> There was a terrific explosion and a large column of water was thrown into the air by the second explosion, flooding the whole bridge. The ship immediately listed to starboard, righted herself and then settled well down by the head.
>
> No. 1 hold flooded immediately, No. 3 hatch was burst open and the deck was cracked across from amidships to the ship's side. Oil was coming from No. 3 tank to the surface, and on the bridge I found bags of boneless beef which I think had been blown through the hole made by the torpedo in the ship's side.

It was the enterprising Werner Witte with U-509 again. Taking advantage of the poor visibility, he had closed in to point blank range before firing. With the *Corinaldo* all but hove-to in the pounding seas it would have been difficult for him to have missed.

It was obvious to Captain Anderson that, being holed in two places and with ominous cracks appearing in her deck plating, his ship would not stay afloat for long. On the other hand, abandoning ship in the weather prevailing was something best left until all hope had gone. With the sea pouring into her breached holds, the *Corinaldo* had ceased to ride the waves, and was simply wallowing in the troughs. Then Chief Engineer Magnus Peterson appeared on the bridge. He reported to Anderson that the main engines and boilers were undamaged, but the watertight bulkhead between No. 3 hold and the stokehold was badly buckled and looked to be about to collapse. If that happened, the engine room would be immediately flooded, and that would be the end of the *Corinaldo*. It was time to go.

When Anderson reached the boat deck, he found that his orders had been anticipated, and three of the *Corinaldo*'s four lifeboats were on the point of being lowered. A glance over the side told him that although the engines had been stopped, the ship still had considerable way on her, which would make launching the boats a very hazardous operation. He attempted to call a halt to the launching, but two of the boats were already on their way down. It was more by good luck than skilful handling that they managed to clear the ship's side without being swamped or capsized. The third boat was held in the davits until the ship was completely stopped.

Accompanied by Chief Officer G. Clark, Captain Anderson then searched the ship for any others who might be on board. The search revealed seven men, fortunately none of them injured. These Anderson sent to the boat deck with Chief Officer Clark, then he went back alone to take a final look around. This yielded no more survivors, but when Anderson returned to the boat deck he found that the last boat had gone, leaving him on board with Clark and the seven others. He later wrote in his report:

> Having satisfied myself that no one remained on board I returned aft and at 2055 GMT left the ship on the starboard raft with the remainder of the crew. We had great difficulty in getting clear of the vessel as she was drifting so fast to leeward. We eventually managed to get clear and worked the raft into the oil slick which the vessel was leaving. Before getting into the slick the seas were breaking over the raft, making it very uncomfortable, but once in the slick we were all right.

We were on the raft until 2345 when we were picked up by HMS *Cowslip*. When we got on board I found that most of my crew had been picked up by her. No. 2 boat was missing, but eventually arrived in Funchal on 9th November. No. 1 boat was capsized by the heavy seas when it came alongside and twenty of the twenty-four occupants were saved. These men were saved by the bravery of some of the crew of HMS *Cowslip*, who were lowered into the oil covered water with ropes tied round them and hauled the men in the water to safety.

While the last men to leave the *Corinaldo* fought to manoeuvre their life-raft away from the sinking ship, 5 miles astern of the convoy the tanker *Bullmouth* was fighting her own battle with the elements.

The 7,519-ton *Bullmouth*, owned by the Anglo Saxon Petroleum Company of London and commanded by 31-year-old Captain John Brougham, had finished her tour of duty as fleet tanker in Freetown and was on her way home in ballast. Her destination was the River Tyne for a much-needed dry docking and engine overhaul. Proof of the need of the latter had come just as darkness was falling, when Chief Engineer Arthur Hutton reported to the bridge that he would have to reduce speed, and possibly stop, to carry out emergency repairs. This was the news Captain Brougham had been anticipating for some time, but always hoping it would never come. He impressed on Hutton the need to keep going, pointing out the danger the ship would be in if she dropped out of the convoy, but the needs of the *Bullmouth*'s faltering diesel overruled all argument.

It was to the great credit of the British tanker's engineers that they were able to keep steerage way on her, for if she had wandered off course and broached to in the heavy sea running she would have been completely out of control. As it was, by the change of the watch at 2000, the *Bullmouth* was almost out of sight of the rear ships of SL 125, and dropping further and further astern all the time. Half an hour later, those on the bridge of the tanker were treated to a brilliant display of pyrotechnics when U-509 stopped the *Corinaldo* with two torpedoes.

Captain Brougham took some comfort from the fact that he had been forced to leave the convoy before the attack, but he also knew that where there was one U-boat, there would be others. However, there was little he could do other than to hope that the darkness would hide his ship. For a supposedly non-combatant merchant ship, *Bullmouth* was well armed, mounting a 4.7-inch, a 12-pounder, and six machine guns, and in daylight against visible enemy she would give a good account of herself. At night, threatened by the torpedoes of a hidden U-boat, she would have little chance.

The *Bullmouth* was in fact already under threat. Oberleutnant Hanns-Ferdinand Massmann was in the conning tower of U-409, closing in on the tanker's port quarter and poised to strike his first blow for the German cause. The Type VIIC, commissioned in Danzig by Massmann nine months earlier, was on her first war patrol, as was her commander.

Able Seaman Edward Mann, who was on lookout duty on the upper bridge of the *Bullmouth* from 2100, described subsequent events:

A few minutes later at 2115 I saw lights flashing on our starboard beam. I thought they might be flares dropped by a submarine to attract our attention to starboard, and while we were looking at them, another submarine would attack us on the port side. I turned to the port side to investigate and just as I did so a torpedo struck the ship under the bridge in No. 4 tank on the port side, followed five seconds later by a second torpedo which struck on the same side between No. 1 and 2 tank in the after end of the well deck.

The double explosion was muffled, accompanied by two brilliant flashes and a great gush of water and debris. The tanker lurched over to port, and lay there wallowing in the swell like a beached whale. In an effort to bring her upright again Brougham ordered the starboard tanks to be flooded, but this was to no avail. Ten minutes later, the *Bullmouth* was at 30 degrees to the vertical with the waves crashing over her port bulwarks. Brougham gave the order to abandon ship. There could be no question of lowering boats. The only chance of survival lay with the four life-rafts the tanker carried. Able Seaman Mann later said:

I went forward where several men were trying to free a raft, on which were the Chief Officer and Donkeyman. The ship gave a sudden lurch, the raft freed itself and both men crashed into the water with it.

I went aft, walking along the ship's side, and found a line hanging over, so scaled down this line and eventually got onto this raft followed by some of the crew.

The Captain who was still on deck shouted to us to take the ship's papers and I think one of the men went back for them.

The 3rd Officer who was behind me said he was going back to the bridge with the Captain. The last I saw of the Captain, who is reported missing, was on the bridge.

The two men already on board the raft, Chief Officer Bertram Dickinson and Donkeyman John Smith, had sustained serious injuries when the raft crashed into the sea, Dickinson having several broken ribs and internal injuries, and Smith with a broken shoulder. They were joined by Mann, Able Seaman Frederick Walters, and five of the ship's DEMS gunners, who jumped overboard. Between them, the seven uninjured men succeeded in manoeuvring the raft away from their crippled ship, which appeared to be in danger of capsizing at any moment. At first light on the 30th, there was no sign of the *Bullmouth*, but later in the morning a ship was sighted floating bottom-up, so it was presumed she had rolled over during the night.

The life-raft had on board an ample supply of water, biscuits, Pemmican and Horlicks tablets; not the best of diets, but sufficient to keep the nine survivors alive for many days. The only man on board with any navigation skills was Chief Officer Dickinson, but he was barely conscious and able to take little interest in events. It was up to the two Able Seamen, Mann and Walters, to try to get the raft to the nearest land, the island of Madeira, roughly 100 miles to the south. The raft was too heavy to paddle, so they were at the mercy of the wind and current. Fortunately, both were in their favour, the wind being steady from the north-east, and the prevailing current flowing south-wards at 7–12 miles a day.

For the next three days the raft drifted slowly southwards, then, on the fourth day, they sighted what appeared to be a dark cloud on the horizon. This slowly became the hard outline of land. It was Madeira, and in the opinion of Edward Mann, between 40 and 50 miles off. They had no means of steering the raft, and they were forced to watch helpless as they drifted past the western end of the island. At daybreak on the 5th, the wind went round to the south-east, and with the help of a makeshift sail the raft began to drift back towards the land. This time, they passed within 2 miles of the western side of Madeira, but were unable to get any closer. Red flares were burned, but there was no response from the shore.

When night came, the survivors lay exhausted and without hope on their raft, eventually falling asleep, only to be rudely awakened at 1 o'clock on the morning of 6 November, when they crashed ashore on a rock-strewn beach. They had landed on the tiny island of Bugio, in the Desertas Group, which lie 10 miles south-south-east of the eastern extremity of Madeira. During the night their raft must have been swept around the northern shore by a local current, and then south-wards to the Desertas.

Ilhas Desertas, a group of three small islands, are uninhabited but occasionally visited by fishermen. By an extraordinary stroke of luck, when the *Bullmouth*'s raft came ashore on Bugio, a group of fishermen were on the island hunting goats. They came across the survivors on the southern shore late that morning. After seven days adrift on the raft, only Mann and Walters were capable of walking, and they accompanied the Portuguese fishermen back to their boats and were taken to Funchal. Next morning, a search party set out from Funchal to find the other survivors. Unfortunately, when the party landed on Bugio they found that Donkeyman John Smith had died of his injuries. Chief Officer Bertram Dickinson died in hospital at Funchal.

It later emerged that U-409's torpedo had not sunk the *Bullmouth*; she was still afloat when U-659 sighted her more than an hour later. For Kapitänleutnant Hans Stock, still smarting from the trouncing he had received when attacking Convoy ON 127 in mid-Atlantic seven weeks earlier, this was a God-sent opportunity to make amends. He moved in on the abandoned tanker to within point blank range, and sent her to the bottom with two torpedoes.

And the agony of the night was not yet ended for SL 125. While Hans Stock was disposing of the *Bullmouth*, the ever-active Werner Witte in U-509 was stalking his potential seventh victim of the attack on the north-bound convoy. He had in his sights the motor vessel *Britanny* in Column 10.

Royal Mail Line's *Britanny*, a 4,772-ton cargo/passenger ship under the command of Captain William Dovell, was on a voyage from Buenos Aires to Liverpool with 7,000 tons of hides, rice and cotton. She carried a total complement of fifty-seven, which included eight DEMS gunners and four civilian passengers.

Witte used a single torpedo to dispose of the *Britanny*. She went down quickly, and in abandoning ship twelve crew members, one gunner and one passenger lost their lives. Captain Dovell, thirty-two of his crew, seven gunners and three passengers were picked up by HMS *Kelantan*, which in her newly assigned role of rescue ship was following in the wake of the convoy.

HMS *Kelantan*, a fraction over 900 tons gross, flat bottomed and with the freeboard of a Thames barge, was gradually losing her fight against the wind and sea. Assigned to the role of convoy rescue ship, she was bringing up the rear of SL 125, still in sight of the back markers, but dropping further back all the time as her pathetically inadequate engine struggled to hold her head up into the rough seas. Although accustomed to the less troubled waters of the Indian and Pacific Oceans, Lieutenant Jones and his crew had made every effort to keep in touch with the convoy, but they were fighting a battle they could not win. When the sun rose on the 17th they found themselves alone on an empty and extremely hostile sea.

In her previous life the *Kelantan* had plied the coasts and rivers of the Malaysian peninsular for the Straits Steamship Company, a feeder ship for ocean-going liners in Singapore, and lifeline for rubber planters and their workers. When war came to the Far East in December 1941, she had been requisitioned by the Navy, and metamorphosed into an armed patrol vessel, with a 4-inch gun on her forecastle and machine guns on her tiny bridge. In her new guise as convoy rescue ship she had not been re-equipped in any way, other than with a few scrambling nets and orders to sweep up after the U-boats.

As the tempo of the battle for SL 125 increased, victims of the sinkings began to appear out of the night, lifeboats under oars, aimlessly drifting rafts, and men in the water, red lifejacket lights bobbing on the waves. The *Kelantan* had put her scrambling nets over the side, and was soon dragging survivors on board. Many of them half-naked and covered in the black fuel oil that had leaked from the tanks of their broken ships, they were a heart-rending sight. Most were so shocked and exhausted that they were incapable of pulling themselves up by the scrambling nets, and Lieutenant Jones called for volunteers to go into the water to help them. Ropes were dropped over the side, and the slippery, oil-covered men were hauled aboard onto the rescue ship's deck. It was a rough and brutal business, but time was running out for these people.

In the midst of this frenzied effort to save lives, the *Kelantan*'s steering gear failed, and with lifeboats and rafts bumping alongside she drifted helpless, beam-on to the pounding seas. Rescue work was suspended.

The *Kelantan*'s steering gear was of the antiquated rod & chain system, whereby the helm on the bridge was connected to the steering engine aft by chains running along the deck. Weakened by the unending struggle to hold the ship on course in the heavy seas, one of the chains had snapped, and it required every available man of the little ship's crew working for the next four hours to secure and repair it.

In an interview recorded for the BBC long after the war, Able Seaman Albert Mellor recalled:

> When we eventually started on our way again and got back up top it was dark and we thought 'Oh Christ what's gone on', because all around us as far as the eye could see there were all kinds of lights from boats, rafts and lifeboats. We started to pick up survivors again and realised that they must have been from ships in our convoy.
>
> A lot of ships went down with that particular convoy.
>
> At one time we were picking up survivors there were bales of cotton floating and we saw this fellow on one, he was naked I think he'd been in the shower or something when his ship was torpedoed. Anyway when we got him on board he was already dead. We found out later that he was a chief steward. Well we put him on the promenade deck, because we didn't have time to do anything else. We had a small promenade deck on this boat. It was like a small tugboat. A few hours later I was going around the deck and I saw this fellow just lying on the deck. I'd forgotten about the chief steward and I said, 'Hey mate you can't stay here', and I suddenly realised who it was. It made me feel terrible.

The body on the *Kelantan*'s promenade deck was that of 52-year old Chief Steward Francis May of the *Britanny*.

With her rudder once more answering to the helm, *Kelantan* returned again to her errand of mercy, which went on until daylight came on the 30th. By that time she had in the region of 300 survivors on board from various torpedoed ships, and every spare inch of her accommodation and deck was taken up by cold, wet, oil-covered men, some of them injured. The *Kelantan* carried no doctor, so any first aid rendered was very basic. She had completely lost touch with the convoy, and had no hope of rejoining. Lieutenant Jones sent a signal to the Admiralty requesting permission to land the survivors at Gibraltar, but this was refused, and he was ordered to continue in the wake of the convoy to British waters.

As the *Kelantan* crowded on all speed in a renewed effort to rejoin the convoy, the *Corinaldo*, her hull ripped open by Witte's torpedoes, was drifting astern, alone and deserted by her crew. Battered by fierce rain squalls, listing heavily to port, and rolling drunkenly beam-on to the long Atlantic swell, the crippled ship was spilling her precious cargo of Argentinian beef into the sea. Hungry sharks circled around her, darting in from time to time to tear at the floating carcasses.

In the very early hours of the 30th, the abandoned ship was found by Hans Stock, who in U-569 was on his way to join in the savaging of SL 125. The helpless *Corinaldo* offered the ideal opportunity for Stock to open his score, but it was not to be that easy. Despite being hit by another brace of torpedoes at close range, the *Corinaldo* stubbornly refused to sink. Stock gave up in disgust and moved on.

Two hours passed, then Hermann Kottmann in U-203 came across the waterlogged wreck, and finally put an end to her misery. A single torpedo, the fifth to blast its way into the *Corinaldo*'s exposed hull, failed to sink her, and Kottmann then took the risk of using his deck gun to put her down. What passed for dawn in that storm-wracked sea was beginning to pale the eastern sky before the *Corinaldo* finally surrendered to the deep.

The *Kelantan* never did rejoin her convoy. She sailed on alone and unmolested for 2,000 miles through U-boat infested waters, finally berthing in Greenock on 8 November. Not surprisingly, with more than ten times her normal complement on board, she ran out of food long before she reached the Clyde. The survivors were taken off on arrival, and the *Kelantan*, her engines exhausted by the long haul, was towed into Greenock. The local fish & chip shop made good money that night.

CHAPTER THIRTEEN

Panic Stations

The night of the 29th had ended on a high note for the U-boats, with the *Britanny*, the *Bullmouth* and the *Corinaldo* being consigned to watery graves, along with 12,273 tons of cargo and twenty-eight men. The convoy had now lost eight ships in seventy-two hours, and still the end of the nightmare was not in sight. Lieutenant Commander Rayner was at his wit's end. Keeping radio silence had become irrelevant, and he sent yet another signal to the Admiralty asking for help. Again nothing. And now things were about to get worse. The U-boats had reloaded their tubes and were back, with U-604 in the van.

From the time he first sighted the damaged tanker *Anglo Maersk* on the morning of the 27th, it had taken Horst Höltring thirteen hours and nine of U-604's arsenal of torpedoes to sink her. This had been a costly exercise, and meanwhile Höltring had lost touch with SL 125. Late that night, having watched the stubborn tanker go to her last resting place, he had then set off after the convoy. The weather at the time was fair, with a light NNW'ly breeze and slight sea. Overhead, the cloud had broken to reveal a bright moon that enhanced the already good visibility.

Despite running on the surface at 10 knots, it was not until sunset on the 29th that the rear ships of SL 125 came in sight, by which time the weather had taken a serious turn for the worse. The wind had backed to the WNW, and was blowing force 6-7, with a rough breaking sea and a high swell. The sky was heavily overcast, and loaded with rain, which from time to time swept across in fierce driving squalls. For Kapitänleutnant Höltring, keeping vigil in U-604's conning tower with the men of the watch, life was far from comfortable. He remarked in his log, 'Holding contact very difficult due to the sea state, heavy rain squalls.' This was a mixed blessing, for although it was difficult to keep his quarry in view, the weather also served to hide the U-boat from the convoy's escorts. Remaining on the surface, diving occasionally to listen with his hydrophones, Höltring cautiously overtook the convoy on its port side. He was adopting the usual tactic, planning to take up position ahead, and let the ships come to him. Unfortunately, the visibility was so poor, that at some time during the night he lost contact with his intended victims.

The 30th dawned with the cloud down to mast-top height, the wind being steady in the north-west and blowing gale force. Unwilling to risk staying on the surface, Höltring took U-604 down to periscope depth. He did an all-round sweep of the horizon and, much to his surprise, he sighted the leading ships of the convoy on his starboard quarter. Conspicuous, in the head of the centre column, was a large, high-sided passenger vessel. She was, Höltring estimated, a ship of at least 11,000 tons, and might well be a troopship. He entered in his log:

08.00 NW 6, Sea 5–6, 1013 mb,
17.5°C, Cloudy.
08.59 Convoy in sight bearing 150° T. Held contact on mastheads and manoeuvred ahead. Contact holding on the control room periscope has proved itself very well as in previous cases, above all in the rough sea. The biggest ship seen so far is the foremost ship in the middle column.

The target that caught Höltring's attention was the 11,898-ton troop transport *Président Doumer*, stationed at the head of SL 125's fourth column.

The *Président Doumer*, launched in 1933 for the prestigious French company *Messageries Maritimes* to carry passengers and mail on their Marseilles–Suez–Madagascar service, had had an inauspicious start to her career, going straight to a lay-by berth after being launched, and there she mouldered for two years during the worldwide economic depression. She eventually went into service in June 1935, but her maiden voyage was cut short when she was forced to put into Aden for engine repairs. She returned to Marseilles, where she spent another five months under repair. Thereafter, she made regular voyages between Marseilles and the Indian Ocean carrying passengers and cargo. When France went to war in 1939, she was requisitioned by the French Navy for service as a troopship, and in April 1940 she was engaged in the ill-fated Allied attempt to free Norway.

Three months later, after the capitulation of France, the *Président Doumer* was seized by the Royal Navy in the Suez Canal and handed over to the Ministry of War Transport for service as a troopship under the management of Bibby Line of Liverpool. Her French master, Captain Jean Paul Mantelet, elected to stay with his ship, as did seventy-four of his crew, including most of his French officers, the remainder being repatriated to France. Ninety British Indian ratings were put on board to make up the numbers, along with fifteen gunners and three signallers from the Royal Navy.

When Japan came into the war, the *Président Doumer* was employed as a troop transport in the Indian Ocean, and was on her way home with SL 125 for dry-docking and repairs. In addition to her crew of 260, she had on board eighty-five passengers, mainly military personnel.

Deciding it would be unwise to attack in daylight, Höltring patiently stalked his intended prey, surfacing after dark and moving close in. The entries in his log read:

> 20.40 With the beginning of twilight ran slowly towards the convoy. Took aim at the fattest one from the day. The first thing that comes in sight after the beginning of twilight is our fat one.
>
> 21.29 2-fan. Both hit from 800 metres. Afterwards great fire-works. Steamer, about 11,000 GRT. Large passenger steamer with low smoke stack, of type like *Abosso* of the Elder Steamer Line.
>
> This type was independently found by those who saw the steamer from 'Merchant Ships 1940'.

Coincidentally, Elder Dempster Line's 11,330-ton *Abosso* had been sunk less than twenty-four hours earlier by U-575 in mid-Atlantic while sailing alone from Cape Town to Liverpool. At that time she had on board a total complement of 393, of which her master Captain Reginald Tate, 149 of his crew, eighteen naval gunners and 193 passengers were lost.

Although the *Président Doumer* was on full alert following the savaging of the convoy on the previous day, no one on board was aware that she was being stalked by U-604, and that at dusk Horst Höltring was within half a mile of the ship. The torpedoing of the troopship brought an immediate response from nearby ships. Rockets and flares soared into the air, at least one ship opened fire with her 4-inch, and another, the ex-Danish *Tasmania*, stationed astern of the stricken ship, dropped one of the two depth charges she carried. Once again, confusion reigned.

Höltring's torpedoes struck the *Président Doumer* squarely in her engine room, causing an immediate loss of power. All lights on board failed, and she began to settle quickly by the stern. Eye-witnesses stated that much of the liner's bridge and accommodation beneath was completely destroyed. In which case, it must be assumed that the majority of her officers were killed. This could account for the ensuing confusion.

Leaderless and frightened, the *Président Doumer*'s largely Indian crew flew into a blind panic and rushed for the boats. With the ship in complete darkness and rolling beam-on to the swell, launching the stricken ship's eight large lifeboats called for clear thinking and expert seamanship, none of which, in the absence of the French officers, seems to have been in evidence. Improperly launched, boat after boat fell 50 feet to the water below. Some were empty, others had just a few men in them. It seems that most of the survivors had jumped or fallen overboard, and the heavy boats crashed down on them, causing a bloody carnage that attracted shoals of voracious sharks. What should have been an orderly evacuation – the *Président Doumer* took fifteen minutes to go down – turned into a disaster.

Captain Berge Mevatne of the Norwegian steamer *Alaska*, in the adjacent column, stated that the torpedoed ship remained upright and, in his opinion, there should have been no difficulty in launching all her lifeboats. Instead, most people fell or jumped overboard, the majority of them without lifejackets. Those who managed to get into the lifeboats were 'like wild cats from panic, and fought with knives and oars to keep their place in the boat and prevent others from entering.'

The 5,681-ton *Alaska*, built in Vancouver at the end of the First World War for Furness Withy Line of London, had been sold to Christian Haaland of Norway in 1921. Commanded by Captain Berge Mevatne, she was on a voyage from Colombo to London with a cargo of tea and other produce, and had taken bunkers and stores in Cape Town before joining SL 125 at Freetown. Captain Mevetne later described the rescue of the *Président Doumer* survivors:

> The sea was thick with swimming and drifting people, with or without lifebelts, screaming for help. About thirty men of *Alaska*'s crew were standing by the railings on both sides to haul survivors on board, but as none of them made any effort to tie the lines around themselves, the Norwegians had to get into the water to assist those who were too exhausted. A few were pulled on board in this manner, but these efforts were gradually given up because of the dangers involved due to the high seas and all the sharks along the side of the ship. A ruined lifeboat with forty-eight people was alongside, none of whom were able to climb the ladder, so the 2nd and 3rd mates went down in the boat and after

a short period of time they had fastened lines around forty-six of them, whereupon they were hauled aboard the *Alaska* by willing hands. The remaining two were crushed between the side of the lifeboat and the ship because they were hanging outside the boat.

In all, thanks mainly to the efforts of Second Mate Engel Thuen and Third Mate Georg Aschehoug, the *Alaska* snatched fifty-six men from the sea, few of whom showed any gratitude to their rescuers. Twenty-nine others were picked up by the corvette *Cowslip*. Of the remainder of the *Président Doumer*'s complement of 345, Captain Jean Paul Mantelet and 259 others were missing, later to be declared dead.

The 6,405-ton motor vessel *Tasmania* was following up astern of the *Président Doumer* when she was so brutally dispatched by U-604. For Captain Hans Christian Roder, who had already taken a huge risk in stopping to pick up forty-four survivors from the sunken *Hopecastle*, witnessing the demise of the big troop transport was the straw that broke the proverbial camel's back. He rang for full speed and altered onto a NW'ly course to run clear of the convoy. As he passed the sinking trooper, he dropped a single depth charge, more to relieve his frustration than in the hope of blowing the hidden U-boat out of the water.

The *Tasmania*, owned by Orient D/S A/S of Copenhagen, was another exiled ship requisitioned by the Admiralty. She had been put under the management of T. & J. Brocklebank of Liverpool, but continued to trade as normal to India and the Far East. On her current voyage, she was carrying a heavy load of 2,000 tons of pig iron and 400 tons of ore, along with 6,100 tons of tea and jute. Not one cubic foot of her cargo space remained unfilled, and her Plimsoll Mark was all but submerged.

As she worked up to full speed, the *Tasmania* shouldered aside the rough head seas with apparent ease, corkscrewing from trough to crest in a cloud of blown spray. She made a brave sight, but when she began to pound and bury her forecastle head in the waves, Captain Roder was obliged to give thought to his valuable cargo. He reduced to half speed, which at 9 knots was still 2 knots faster than the convoy. Once clear of the other ships, Roder intended to resume a more northerly course, and with the wind and sea on the port bow, increase speed again.

That was the plan, but as so often happens, the best laid plans can go astray. And so it was for the *Tasmania*. At five minutes before 7 o'clock, less than half an hour after the *Président Doumer* was torpedoed, U-659 appeared out of the night.

Hans Stock, who twenty-four hours earlier had failed to sink the *Corinaldo*, but had managed to despatch the abandoned *Bullmouth*, had reloaded his tubes and was seeking a more challenging target. He was delighted when the shadow he had been stalking turned out to be a heavily loaded ship, and a lone runner to boot. He moved in closer, and fired a two spread from his bow tubes. Chief Officer A. Pedersen described what happened when one of Stock's torpedoes exploded in the *Tasmania*'s No. 3 hold:

> There was a dull explosion and a huge column of water was thrown up. No one saw the track of the torpedo and no flash was seen from the explosion. The vessel listed heavily to port but righted herself almost at once, and started to settle by the stern. A large hole was visible in the ship's side, and I think the bulkhead between Nos 3 and 4 holds had collapsed. The engines were stopped and a wireless distress message was sent out. Orders were given to abandon ship and our two lifeboats were manned and lowered; one of the rafts was released and about eight men managed to get on to it, leaving twelve men, including myself, on board. It was then decided to launch the heavy raft which was stowed on top of the awning spars on the port side of the bridge deck; this was a very difficult job as the raft was not placed on skids and had to be partly lifted, but eventually it was safely launched and ten of the remaining twelve men on board jumped on to it. The missing Chief Engineer and Army Gunner Lee refused to jump on to the raft although they had plenty of time to do so, but I learned later that Lee did attempt to jump, but misjudged the distance, and fell amongst the chests of tea and debris which was floating about, and was probably killed. The raft drifted away from the ship, and with the exception of these two men, all the crew were clear by 1940.

The sudden and calamitous end of the *Président Doumer*, quickly followed by the torpedoing of the *Tasmania*, sent shock waves rippling throughout the convoy. After five horror-filled days and nights under attack, during which eight ships had been hit and abandoned, nerves were on a knife edge, and many of the ships still unharmed were seriously contemplating breaking ranks and making a full-speed dash for home. But despite the fraught situation, no less than four ships went to the aid of the *Président Doumer* and the *Tasmania*. The Norwegian steamer *Alaska*, and the British ships *Baron Elgin* and *Baron Vernon*, all reversed course and went back to pick up survivors. The Dutch-owned, British-flag *Mano*, the smallest ship in the convoy at a mere 1,418 tons, and sailing as rear ship of Column 3, also moved in to pick up survivors. Unfortunately, in trying to get alongside the *Mano*, one of the *Tasmania's* lifeboats capsized under her stern, throwing all its occupants into the water. The *Mano* picked up some of the survivors, while the *Baron Elgin* took the rest on board.

First on the scene was the 3,642-ton *Baron Vernon*, one of the 'Hungry Hogarths' Baron Line of Glasgow. She was deep-loaded with 5,400 tons of ore, loaded at an anchorage off Pepel Island, 14 miles upriver from Freetown. This was not the ideal cargo to carry in time of war – a cargo that could send her to the bottom like a stone should she be torpedoed. However, this did not deter her master, Captain Peter Liston from going to the help of the ships in need. He later wrote in a report to the Admiralty:

> At approximately 1920 on 30 October the *Président Doumer*, five cables on our starboard beam, was hit by a torpedo and sheered towards us, apparently out of control. To avoid collision, I ordered hard to port, and steadied the vessel on a course of 30 degrees from the original; columns 1 and 2 followed my example. The rest of the convoy carried straight on, although we had instructions to make an alteration to port of 30° at this time. Between a quarter of an hour and half an hour later, the *Tasmania*, on my port bow, was torpedoed, and as she was unable to send off her signal rockets, I did so for her. We were slightly astern of this ship, and coming up towards her beam I found two of her rafts and her lifeboat loaded with men. There was a heavy swell running with a breaking crest. I had just manoeuvred my ship in order to bring the rafts alongside, when at 2050 on 30th October, whilst in position 36° 06' N 16° 59' W, on a course of 330°, proceeding at a speed of 7 knots, a torpedo struck my ship. There was a very rough sea with a NW Wind, Force 6. The weather was slightly overcast, but visibility was very good.

After torpedoing the *Président Doumer*, Höltring had taken U-604 deep and allowed the convoy to pass over her. Masked by the threshing of the merchantmen's propellers, she escaped detection, and the only retaliation she experienced was the solitary depth charge dropped at random by the *Tasmania*. An hour passed before Höltring deemed it safe to return to the surface. The convoy was now some 10 miles ahead, and visible in the light of snowflakes being fired. Höltring increased to full speed, intending to strike again while confusion still reigned.

The long pursuit proved unnecessary when a ship suddenly loomed up out of the darkness ahead, on an opposite course and steaming slowly. It was the *Baron Vernon* searching for survivors. As she neared the U-boat, Höltring fired a single torpedo at close range.

The torpedo almost missed its mark, striking home right aft, under the *Baron Vernon*'s stern. Her propeller and rudder were blown off, and her poop housing smashed, its shattered remains left hanging over the side. The crippled steamer's engine shuddered to a sudden halt, and all her lights went out. An examination by torchlight of the damage showed that the watertight bulkhead between the two after holds had collapsed, and both holds and the engine room were flooding. Captain Liston, fearing that the ship was about to break in two, ordered his crew to take to the boats.

The *Baron Vernon* was equipped with two large lifeboats and a small jolly boat, each of the full-sized boats being designed to carry fifty-two men. Not surprisingly, the ship being in complete darkness and rolling and pitching in the rough seas, the falls of the starboard lifeboat jammed as it was being lowered, and it had to be abandoned. Fortunately, the port boat went down without a hitch, with most of the crew on board and the Chief Officer in charge. Captain Liston, reluctant to leave until he was certain his ship was sinking, remained on board with the Third Officer. Within ten minutes it became obvious that the waterlogged ship would not remain afloat much longer, and Liston called the lifeboat back alongside. Both men then jumped into the boat, making a soft landing on the shoulders of the occupants.

Under the direction of Captain Liston, the heavily loaded boat then pulled clear of the ship, but as it did so a flashing light was seen on the deck of the sinking ship, and it was discovered that the Radio Officer and three others were still on board. Liston took the lifeboat back and called to the stranded men to jump into the water. This they refused to do. However, at that point a life-raft from the *Tasmania* drifted past, and the four men were able to board. Captain Liston later wrote:

> My crew behaved extraordinarily well, but they were inclined to be a little panicky in the boat at first, until I pointed out that

our hopes of surviving depended upon our keeping calm, and after this there was no further trouble. I hove to, to windward, using the sea anchor and keeping her head to sea, and three hours later the *Baron Elgin* appeared, and picked us up. We manoeuvred alongside, and climbed up the ladders. I told the Captain about my men on the rafts, and he carried out a search for them, eventually picking them up with eleven of the crew from the *Tasmania* and five from the *Hopecastle*. I would like to pay a tribute to the Captain of the *Baron Elgin*, who did splendid work in picking up the survivors.

I did not see my ship sink, as I lost consciousness when I got on board the *Baron Elgin*, but the Captain told me she sank at 2345. She appeared to break in two as she sank, and there was a flash, as if something had blown up. The *Baron Elgin* took us to Madeira, where we arrived the following evening, October 31st, at 1800.

Following close in the wake of the *Baron Vernon* had come her Glaswegian cousin *Baron Elgin*, with Captain James Cameron on the bridge. Slightly larger than the *Baron Vernon* at 4,105 tons gross, the *Baron Elgin* had been built in the same yard on the Clyde. Alerted by the *Président Doumer*'s frantic distress calls, she had come to help clear up the carnage left by the U-boats. As she neared the sea of debris left by the torpedoed ships, her lookouts sighted a man in the water, and she stopped to pick him up. Although the weather was showing signs of moderating, the sea was still very rough, and saving this man proved to be difficult. The *Baron Elgin* was hove-to for forty minutes, during which time a surfaced U-boat was seen to be circling the ship at a distance. Was she manoeuvring to torpedo the *Baron Elgin*? Faced with this dilemma, Captain Cameron was tempted to abandon the rescue attempt, but his humanitarian instinct prevailed. He ordered his gunners to keep the enemy in their sights, but unless the U-boat attacked, to hold their fire. He carried on with the rescue, picking up forty men from one of the *Tasmania*'s lifeboats, and the *Baron Vernon*'s entire crew of forty-nine. All the time the U-boat continued to circle without attempting to interfere. This was taken to be a very generous gesture on the part of the U-boat commander. The contrary was true.

In fact, Horst Höltring – for it was U-604 – was all the time making strenuous efforts to sink the *Baron Elgin*. When the British ship first appeared, steaming at slow speed, Höltring was somewhat taken aback by the number of easy targets being presented to him. He first tried a quick shot from his bow tubes, but the torpedo was a rogue, sinking deep before it reached its target. A second torpedo fired a few minutes later, the last remaining in U-604's bow tubes, ran well, but Höltring had miscalculated the *Baron Elgin*'s speed and it sailed across her bows with yards to spare.

Höltring had just one torpedo left, and this was in U-604's stern tube. After two frustrating misses he decided to save this for a more worthwhile target, and with SL 125 in total disarray there were plenty on offer. Captain Cameron, still unaware that his ship was under attack, continued to search for survivors. At midnight, still unmolested, the *Baron Elgin*, with eighty-nine survivors on board, including sixteen of the *Hopecastle*'s crew the *Tasmania* had rescued, set course for Madeira at full speed.

When the penultimate day of October finally came to a close, SL 125, under sustained attack, had lost ten ships and 44,310 tons of cargo. The voyage was turning into a complete rout, and Lieutenant Commander John Rayner and his pitifully small escort force of four corvettes could do nothing to stop it. Lieutenant Holm, commanding HMS *Crocus*, later wrote:

> Asdic contacts were made by all the escorts at various times and many depth charges were dropped. Down they went, then up in a tremendous cloud of water and spray that obscured all around it. It is likely that some U-boats were damaged or even destroyed but in this unsatisfactory and largely unseen warfare we did not know ... Commander Newey (*sic.*) had come to the conclusion that one of the enemy's tactics was to submerge before dark and, perhaps using their periscopes, get in to such a position that the convoy came over on top of them. They could then surface after dark and fire torpedoes at will and at point blank range, without much chance of missing. This at the same time would render the defensive guns of the convoy ships virtually useless, for two reasons. Often the guns could not depress far enough and even if they could, the chances were that if they opened fire they would have hit one of their colleagues. They could, of course, and did use machine guns, and these no doubt killed a few Germans and certainly prevented them from coming out of the conning tower to get to their big gun, but the machine guns had no effect on their ability to fire torpedoes. The added bonus in this U-boat strategy was that our most valuable ships were usually in the centre of the

convoy. After doing their damage the U-boats could either dive and hope to avoid our inadequate escort screen or, with their superior speed, escape on the surface.

To counter these tactics, *Petunia* took station one night right in the middle of the convoy. Sure enough, as Newey (*sic.*) expected, a U-boat surfaced almost ahead of him. *Petunia* gave chase with a speed just about matching that of the surfaced U-boat and, at the same time, told *Cowslip* by radio telephone that the U-boat was coming out his side of the convoy.

Cowslip, commanded by Lieutenant Frederick Granger, RNR, had spotted the U-boat, and immediately gave chase, but as she did she began to experience serious boiler problems and was forced to reduce speed and break off the pursuit. At midnight, she signalled to *Petunia* that her engineers were unable to solve the problem, and she was making for Gibraltar at her best speed, which was then 5 knots.

When daylight came on the 31st, it was apparent that SL 125 was in a perilous state. Lieutenant Holm commented:

> We were reduced to twenty-six ships in a convoy spread over many miles of ocean. There were now only three escorts. I had the Commodore on board *Crocus* and the Vice Commodore had gone with his ship *Stentor*. There were many gaps in the ranks, many stragglers, so obviously some reforming was necessary. *Petunia* called on her two remaining ships *Woodruff* and *Crocus* to help with the passing of messages and, like a sheepdog with a flock, rounded up the ships into lines. By dark we looked something like a convoy again, with one escort trying to cover the front of about 3 miles and the others covering a side each. We even had a new acting Commodore, the Captain of one of the merchant ships.

Admiral Dönitz's War Diary had a different tale to tell:

> On the morning of 31.10 convoy lay in CF 96 (340 miles WSW of Cape St Vincent) with NNE course and speed 7 knots. Convoy appeared to pass Gibraltar and continued northwards. With the wind dropping from west and sea strength 3-4 contact was maintained by U-604 and U-509. By afternoon the six boats of the group had come up with the convoy. In the morning U-509 and U-604 had reported that all that remained of the convoy was four to five ships. In the afternoon, U-604 reported there were certainly twelve.

Quite a number of the merchantmen in SL 125 were 13 or 14 knotters, and in view of the totally inadequate escort force, the temptation for them to leave the convoy and press on at full speed must have been great. One ship that succumbed was the 6,373-ton motor vessel *Silverwillow*, which had a service speed of 13½ knots. When the battle was at its height, her master Captain Reginald Butler, confident that his twin diesel engines would give 15 knots if pushed, had quietly peeled away from the convoy and vanished into the night, but not before she had been spotted by HMS *Crocus*. Lieutenant Holm ordered her to rejoin the convoy, but Butler refused. A short while later, Holm reported seeing a flash followed by an explosion, and wrote the *Silverwillow* off as 'another statistic'.

CHAPTER FOURTEEN

The Last Miles

The *Silverwillow* had been leading SL 125's tenth column and, adhering to the Commodore's instructions, breasting the waves at an excruciatingly slow 5 knots. She was all but hove-to. On her bridge, Captain Reginald Butler, sickened by the systematic destruction of the convoy by the U-boats, and horrified by the inability of the escorting corvettes to put a stop to it, had for some time been debating the alternatives open to him. They were few. Either he could continue to stay in line, thereby exposing his ship and crew to sudden death by torpedo, or he could pull out of the convoy and make a run for it alone.

The 6,373-ton *Silverwillow*, owned by the Silver Line of London, was on passage from Lagos to Liverpool with a cargo of 9,000 tons of West African produce, a mixture of palm kernels, groundnuts, sawn timber, bales of raw rubber and two tanks of palm oil in bulk. In addition to her crew of fifty-three, she also had on board eight naval gunners and six passengers. Captain Butler's thoughts were: taking into account the prevailing weather, which must surely soon moderate, the *Silverwillow* should manage at least 12 knots, given her head. That being so, she could reach the comparative safety of the Western Approaches within four days. There were fearful risks involved, but to make a break for it might be preferable to offering an easy target to the U-boats – as his ship was now doing. It was time for a decision to be made.

It is not clear whether the *Silverwillow* did deliberately leave the convoy, but a report by Lieutenant John Holm, commanding the corvette *Crocus*, reads:

> The temptation for a fast ship to go ahead independently was too strong for some to resist. A few of these ships were capable of 15 knots and there was not much comfort for them in SL 125. For some the temptation was too great. One or two, like the *Esperance Bay* and *Amstelkirk*, might have got away with it, but we never knew.
>
> One ship that tried, but succeeded only partly, was *Silverwillow*. On the fourth night of the attack, a U-boat was reported to be on the starboard side of the convoy. *Crocus* was doing her prescribed

search with starshell, Asdic and radar, when we got an echo that seemed too large for a U-boat. We closed and found it to be *Silverwillow*, going flat out by herself to the north-eastward. We had no time to spare so flashed to her 'Rejoin convoy', and got on with our hunt.

Captain Butler did not admit to running away, but wrote in his report to the Admiralty, 'For the time being I had lost touch with the convoy owing to bad visibility.' Whatever happened, the *Silverwillow*'s fate was soon decided for her.

At 25, Oberleutnant-zur-See Hanns-Ferdinand Massmann was one of Dönitz's younger commanders, and an aspiring ace. He had been appointed to his first command, albeit the small coastal boat U-137, at the age of 23, and had soon earned himself the nickname *Hai* (Shark) for his zeal and complete lack of fear when in action. The crew of his second command, U-409, described him as being 'daring almost to the point of recklessness'. However, for all Massmann's daring, his only success with SL 125 so far had been the torpedoing of the tanker *Bullmouth* on the night of 29 October – and she failed to sink. He was consequently more than anxious to live up to his reputation when, in all the confusion accompanying the sinking of the *Président Doumer*, he found the *Silverwillow* alone and vulnerable. Captain Butler's report relates the sequence of events that followed:

> On the night of 30th October at 2010 ATS the *Président Doumer* was struck by a torpedo and a few minutes later when in approximate position 35.00 N 17.00 W we were struck by a torpedo. There was a rough sea and very high swell at the time with NW Force 7, the sky was overcast, with very poor visibility. The degaussing was off and we were proceeding on a Northerly course at a speed of 5 knots. The ship was swinging and for the time being I had lost touch with the convoy owing to bad visibility. The ship appeared to have been hit amidships in No. 3 hold abaft the bridge on the port side in the deep tank.

A deluge of hot palm oil falling on the bridge gave the impression that the *Silverwillow* had been hit in her No. 3 deep tank, which contained palm oil, but in fact Massmann's torpedo had gone home right forward, in the forepeak tank, also full of palm oil.

The *Silverwillow* immediately began to settle by the bow. Her collision bulkhead had collapsed and the sea was pouring into her No. 1

hold. So quickly did she appear to be sinking that Butler ordered his crew to take to the boats. Conditions for this operation were far from ideal. The night was very dark; the ship, being by this time beam-on to wind and sea, was rolling violently, and the wooden boat deck was slippery with palm oil. Inevitably, things went wrong. Captain Butler later reported:

> The two forward boats were washed out of the blocks and swamped by the heavy sea which was running. The ship swung round but the Chief Officer managed to successfully lower the starboard after boat which was not on the weather side, in spite of the heavy sea running. It was much easier to get the port after boat into the water but we experienced great difficulty in getting it away from the ship's side as the ship was drifting on to the boat. Both boats were away from the ship within ten minutes of the torpedoing. I jumped into the sea and was pulled into the starboard boat which later picked up four or five men out of the water.
>
> As the ship did not seem to be sinking rapidly I thought I would try to reboard her. I had about twenty-eight men in my boat and there were about thirty men in the Chief Officer's boat. I had only a few Europeans in my boat, the rest being Chinese who were of very little use. Although the boat was half full of water they just lay in the bottom and remained there, refusing either to bail or row. The ship was drifting rapidly and it took us about four hours before we finally got to leeward of the ship. I examined the ship for about half an hour and consulted with the Chief Officer and we decided that it was too great a risk to attempt to reboard during the dark hours under existing weather conditions.
>
> It was whilst in the boat that I learned from one of the men we had picked up out of the water that the torpedo actually struck the ship forward and not amidships. This man said that as he was washed around the bow he felt himself being drawn into an immense hole in the bow and then he was washed out again. Later when I saw some bales of rubber floating about I knew that the collision bulkhead had given way and that No. 1 lower hold was open to the sea.

Still hoping to reboard at daylight, Butler kept the two lifeboats riding to sea anchors close to the *Silverwillow*, and it was by pure chance that, at about 0200 on the morning of the 31st, HMS *Kelantan* found them. The little rescue ship already had some 300 survivors on board, and was making full speed to rejoin the convoy. When he saw the *Silverwillow*'s boats, Lieutenant Jones was obliged to heave-to, and by 0300 had added another sixty-one survivors to his already over-crowded decks. Captain Butler requested that Jones stay in the region of the drifting ship, so that he might attempt to reboard at daylight, but with so many survivors on board Jones refused to wait. *Kelantan* was already running short of food, water and fuel, and Jones considered it imperative that she join up with the other ships as soon as possible.

Kelantan eventually regained contact with SL 125 on the morning of 1 November, and Captain Butler again appealed for help to save his torpedoed ship. He later wrote:

> As soon as we rejoined the convoy the Captain of the *Kelantan* sent a message to the Commanding Officer of the Senior Escort Vessel informing him that he had on board survivors from the *Silver-willow* and the *Brittany*.
>
> Shortly afterwards he received a message from the Senior Escort Vessel stating that the *Silverwillow* was still afloat and that a corvette was standing by with some survivors. At my request he then sent a message to the Commanding Officer of the Senior Escort Vessel requesting that a corvette might take some of my crew back to the ship as by that time a destroyer and another corvette had joined the convoy. As the weather was still very bad, making boat work out of the question, I even volunteered that if a corvette was placed at our disposal my crew could get aboard by jumping into the sea wearing their life belts and be hauled up.

There seems to be no doubt that Captain Butler was prepared to go to any lengths to salvage his ship, but there is nothing on record to say that any of his officers or crews were prepared to commit themselves to the mercy of the raging seas in the hope that they could somehow clamber aboard the *Silverwillow*. It would be brave men who would attempt such a dangerous exercise, and it must be remembered that those same men had already been through five days under attack, at the culmination of which they had been forced to take to the boats. Lieutenant Commander Rayner, not unreasonably, refused Captain Butler's request.

While this exchange was going on, 60 miles astern of the convoy the Norwegian steamer *Alaska*, appointed as additional rescue ship by the Convoy Commodore, was still searching for more survivors from the disastrous loss of the trooper *Président Doumer*.

Shortly after midnight on the 30th, while the men of the *Silverwillow* were fighting to get their lifeboats clear of the drifting ship, the *Alaska* was stopped and manoeuvring to pick up some men in the water. It was a delicate manoeuvre, calling for seamanship of the highest order. The night was black, the wind howling in the rigging, and the ship rolling drunkenly as the sea and swell surged against her hull. Captain Berg Mevatne was having great difficulty in providing a lee for the survivors to board. No one was watching for the enemy.

Hidden in the darkness to starboard, U-510 was also battling against the turbulent seas. In her conning tower, cold, wet and half-blinded by spray, Korvettenkapitän Karl Neitzel was far from happy. This, his second patrol in command, was turning out to be so different to the first, which had been in the warm and largely untroubled waters of the Caribbean.

In contrast to the young Hanns-Ferdinand Massmann, commanding U-409, at 41, Karl Neitzel was one of the oldest U-boat commanders on active service in the Second World War. He had begun his naval career in the torpedo boats of the Kaiser's navy in 1917, and languished ashore after Germany's ignominious defeat, returning to sea in 1923 to serve in minesweepers of the fledgling *Reichsmarine*. He joined Dönitz's U-boat arm in February 1941, commissioning the Type IXC U-510 in Hamburg in November of that year.

Neitzel's first command began on a bad note when, on 2 August 1942, he sank the Uruguayan steamer *Maldonado* off the coast of South America. The 5,285-ton *Maldonado* was on her way from Montevideo to New York with 7,000 tons of tinned meat. At that time, Uruguay was still neutral, but Neitzel mistook her for a Greek-flag ship, and sent her to the bottom, having first taken her master as a prisoner of war. The incident prompted a strong diplomatic protest by the Uruguayan government to Berlin, and sparked off anti-German demonstrations. Admiral Dönitz was not pleased.

To make amends for his error of judgement in sinking a neutral ship, Karl Neitzel sank two British ships totalling 13,000 tons a few days later. Now he was about to continue his return to grace by sinking the *Alaska*.

Neitzel's torpedo hit the *Alaska* in her No. 1 hold on the starboard side, the resulting explosion being so powerful that it blew the hatch-boards and tarpaulins high in the air, and those on her bridge were knocked off their feet. The ship began to dip by the head, and within minutes her foredeck was awash. Captain Mevatne stopped his engines, ordered the wireless room to send out a distress, and made preparations for abandoning ship. He then went down to the officers' saloon where Second Mate Engel Thuen and Steward Trygve Hansen were tending to injured survivors from the *Président Doumer*. Seven men had already died of their wounds, while two more had serious head injuries. Mevatne described the saloon as looking like 'a butcher's house' where they were 'wading in blood'.

Captain Mevatne went next to the boat deck, where he found complete panic, generated mainly by the able-bodied survivors from the *Président Doumer*. They had rushed the boats, two of which were already on their way down to the water. With the help of some of *Alaska*'s crew, Mevatne restored order, and the two starboard boats were safely lowered, each with twenty-five men on board. Chief Mate Finn Johansen had charge of the motor lifeboat, and with him were Chief Engineer John Natvig and *Alaska*'s radio officer, along with the lifeboat radio. Johansen was instructed to hold the boats alongside while Captain Mevatne assessed the damage to the ship. An attempt had been made to launch the port side boats, but due to the heavy starboard list and the rough seas, this ended in disaster, with one of the boats being smashed against the ship's side. Fortunately, none of the crews were thrown into the water, the ship by now being sur-rounded by sharks.

A thorough inspection of the ship revealed that although the *Alaska* was partly waterlogged and listing heavily, her engines were intact and she appeared to be in no immediate danger of sinking. Mevatne called the lifeboats back alongside, and despite the big sea running, they were hoisted back on board. The emergency boiler was flashed up, and by pumping ballast aft and jettisoning cargo forward, the ship was brought reasonably upright and on an even keel. Course was then set for Madeira, some 200 miles to the south.

The corvette *Cowslip*, which had dropped out of the convoy on the 30th with boiler problems, was limping northwards towards Gibraltar when she came across the *Silverwillow*, abandoned by her crew but still afloat. The story is taken up by Captain William Anderson of the British ship *Corinaldo*, torpedoed and sunk by U-509 on the night of 29 October. Anderson and forty-nine of his crew were survivors on board the *Cowslip*:

> At daylight on the 31st we sighted a ship on the horizon. The com-
> mander sent for me to see if I could recognise her. I said I thought

she was the *Silverwillow*. Whilst proceeding towards her we came across an upturned boat with two men in it, a Chinaman and a naval rating from the *Silverwillow*. We took them on board and soon afterwards sighted another lifeboat with sail hoisted. We made towards it and discovered the Second Officer, Steward and an AB from the *Tasmania*. We took these men on board and on nearing this ship discovered she was the *Silverwillow* and that she had been abandoned. I called for volunteers to board her and nineteen immediately volunteered. I selected eight of my crew and three from the *Tasmania* and went aboard to inspect her. I found that the torpedo had struck in No. 1 hold, which was flooded and that the rest of the ship was dry, all soundings being normal. We tried to get the engines going and worked on them for a long time. We got the generators going and filled the after peak tank through hoses with small motor pumps to try and lift the ship's head.

Cowslip's problems had been compounded when, while she was screening the torpedoed ships, she picked up another forty-seven survivors from the *Président Doumer*. With this addition, the tiny corvette had a total of 223 survivors on board, some of whom were injured. It had therefore become imperative that she make port as soon as possible, not only for the injured, but also because her food and water were running dangerously low. Lieutenant Commander Granger was still debating what course of action to take when they came across yet another lifeboat. An official Admiralty news release explains:

When the British corvette HMS *Cowslip* (Lieutenant-Commander F. Granger, RNR) was picking up survivors after a convoy action, the ship was passed by a life-boat sailing at a brisk pace, in the direction of land 600 miles away.

In it were four men. They waved, and continued on their way.

The commanding officer of the corvette, surprised that they showed no desire to be saved, made to come alongside them, but found that the life-boat was making too good a speed, so he signalled them to heave-to.

A Danish Merchant Navy officer from the life-boat came smartly on board the *Cowslip* and reported to the bridge. He said that his ship had been torpedoed, and that his captain and crew had been picked up. He himself had informed the captain that he did not intend to leave the ship, but thought he could do more good by waiting until next morning to look for more survivors. The bo'sun and two sailors had volunteered to stay with him, instead of being picked up.

He said he could make land in five days, and had seventy-five gallons of petrol in reserve. Knowing that the corvette had many survivors on board, he would not impose further on their accommodation.

'It was only when he learned that we had medical cases on board and that he could be of use, having had two years of medical training that he consented to be rescued', said the commanding officer of the corvette. 'He went straight below and spent the rest of the trip looking after them. That is the kind of man you find in the Atlantic.'

It was later revealed that the navigator/medic was the Second Officer of the Danish motor vessel *Tasmania*, torpedoed on the night of 29 October by Hans Stock in U-659.

The salvage tug which had been promised from Gibraltar had not yet arrived, and in consultation with Captain Berge Mevatne, Lieutenant Granger proposed that the *Alaska* should take the *Silverwillow* in tow, at least until the Admiralty tug arrived. This proposal did not appeal to some of the Norwegian ship's crew members. Appalled by the cowardly behaviour of the *Président Doumer* survivors they had picked up, a delegation approached Captain Mevatne stating they would not agree to the tow unless the *Alaska* was stopped at night to allow her crew to take to the boats, reboarding each morning to continue the voyage. If this was not done, they told Mevatne, the entire crew would refuse to work the ship.

Under the circumstances, the fears of *Alaska*'s crew were understandable, but their demands were clearly not. Captain Mevatne's response was to point out to them that if everyone did their duty they still had a chance to save themselves, their ship and her cargo. He also reminded them of their responsibility to the many injured on board, and the dangers involved in lowering boats in the weather prevailing. Nothing more was said, and the *Silverwillow* was taken in tow.

During the afternoon, as ship and tow, with *Cowslip* screening ahead, they inched their way north and met up with a Portuguese passenger vessel which had a doctor on board. Lieutenant Granger, concerned for the injured *Cowslip* and *Alaska* had on board, requested medical assistance, but the Portuguese captain refused to send his doctor across. He proposed that if the injured needed help they must be brought to his ship. This was clearly out of the question, so the ships continued on their separate ways.

Next morning, the weather having moderated, although the swell was still heavy, a lifeboat, manned by Second Mate Engel Thuen and seven of the *Alaska*'s sailors, set out to ferry the more seriously injured of the *Président Doumer*'s survivors across to HMS *Cowslip*. This was an extremely difficult operation, requiring expert boat handling, and it is to the credit of Engel Thuen and his crew that it was successful. Having delivered the injured, they then returned to their ship and took a party of the *Président Doumer*'s engineers over to the *Silverwillow*, where they made strenuous attempts to get the British ship's diesel engines started. The engineers worked round the clock for two days, but without success. By this time the weather was again deteriorating, and Captain Mevatne recalled the boat.

Alaska continued to tow the *Silverwillow* in weather so bad that Mevatne resorted to pouring oil on the sea to ease the strain on the towline. He was greatly relieved when, on the morning of 4 November a signal from the Admiralty to *Cowslip* advised that the salvage tug and escort would arrive soon, and that the two merchantmen would then be taken into Lisbon. Later that day, *Cowslip* reported an engine breakdown, and the ships were once more hove-to. At Lieutenant Granger's request, two of the *Alaska*'s engineers were sent across to the corvette to help with the problem. They returned with broken engine parts, which were then repaired in the Norwegian ship's workshop. *Cowslip* was under way again within two hours.

At the same time, the *Corinaldo*'s men had been busy. Captain Anderson wrote:

> We wirelessed for diesel engineers and tugs and had they arrived I think we should have saved the ship. We were aboard the *Silverwillow* on and off for four days and did everything we could to get her under way. On the evening of 4 November there was 5 feet of water in No. 2 hold and the engine room was flooded. As the weather was very rough we returned to the *Cowslip* for the night and next morning returned with six more of my crew and took off all the light armament. As there was nothing further we could do we proceeded for Gibraltar. On the way we met the tug *Jaunty* escorted by the armed trawler *Leyland* with diesel engineers on board; we turned back with them. On reaching the *Silverwillow* we

were unable to board on account of the bad weather. This weather continued and as the corvette could not wait any longer she left the scene during the night of 5/6 November and proceeded to Gibraltar. The *Alaska* which had been torpedoed was lying close to the *Silverwillow* and during the five days *Cowslip* had screened both vessels and in consequence was running short of fuel.

I would like to recommend the 19 men who volunteered to board the *Silverwillow* with me. The men were on board with me for five days.

Chief Officer G. Clark, Second Officer R. Allan, Second Engineer D. Paterson, First Cook P. Bevans, First Carpenter D. Hutcheson, Able Seaman A. McKellar, Storekeeper R. Wylde.

Ex-*Tasmania*: Steward F. Neilsen, Able Seaman Damsgood, Bosun Christiansen.

The other men who volunteered but whose services were not required until later.

Fourth Engineer E. Hope, Fifth Engineer J. Charlton, Radio Officer C. Humphreys, Steward D. Cossets, Cadet L. Mitchell, Able Seamen W. Foster, Able Seaman J. Busby.

Able Seaman T. Smith, Able Seaman H. McHarg, Trimmer C. Curley and Greaser J. Rogan volunteered but their services were not needed.

On 5 November the salvage tug *Jaunty* took the *Silverwillow* in tow, and with *Alaska* following and the armed trawler *Leyland* screening, headed for Lisbon. The tow went well, until on the 11th, only 90 miles from Lisbon, the weather suddenly worsened, with the wind at gale force, and twelve days after she had been torpedoed the *Silverwillow* succumbed to her wounds and sank. The *Alaska* carried on alone, arriving in Lisbon in the early hours of the morning of 13 November. After temporary repairs, she continued on to a United Kingdom port, and was soon back at sea. Ironically, after the war she was sold to German owners, and after seven years bringing in cargoes to help rebuild the defeated nation, she went to the breaker's yard in 1958 at the grand old age of 40.

Back with SL 125, as darkness fell on the 30th the battered convoy was at last approaching within range of British long-range aircraft based in the south of England and, coincidentally or not, the U-boats appeared to be keeping their distance. The last of the enemy directly involved with SL 125 was Gustav-Adolf Janssen's U-103. At about 2200 on the 30th, Janssen came across the abandoned Danish ship *Tasmania*, and sank her with two torpedoes. When she went down, the *Tasmania* took with her 8,500 tons of tea, jute, pig iron and ores, all a grievous loss to Britain's hard-pressed economy.

In the small hours of 31 October help finally reached SL 125 with the arrival of the two Flower-class corvettes *Coltsfoot* and *Spiraea*. Then, as the coming dawn turned a rain-laden sky from black to grey, the destroyer HMS *Ramsey* came steaming over the horizon. Armed with four 4-inch and two 3-inch guns, torpedo tubes and rack upon rack of depth charges, the 35-knot destroyer, long in the tooth though she might be, was the dashing knight-errant for which SL 125 had waited so long. In command of the ex-US Navy 4-stacker was ex-Orient Line officer, naval reservist Captain Richard Been Stannard VC, RNR. Stannard took command of SL 125's now substantial escort force, thereby lifting a crushing weight from the exhausted Lieutenant Commander John Rayner's shoulders.

All that was needed now for the defence of SL 125 as it entered seriously hostile waters was air support, and this was not yet forthcoming, delayed, it was reported, by the bad weather. But in spite of the weather, German Focke-Wulf Kondors, based in Bordeaux-Merinac, somehow got through. Fortunately, by the time they arrived overhead, the convoy was ready for them. Steaming in tight formation, six columns abreast, and with its reinforced escort around it, SL 125 put up a spirited defence. Lieutenant John Holm later wrote:

> Meanwhile three German bombers had at last found us despite the cloudy weather. Once they knew where we were the weather conditions were of more advantage to them than to us, as they swooped out of the clouds, dropping a bomb or two before taking cover again. This gave us very little time to aim at them before they were obscured. But the convoy and escort showed it had not lost spirit and we combined to put up a good ack-ack barrage. There were some near-misses in the convoy but no hits. The bombers did not even succeed in homing more U-boats on to us, perhaps because of the worsening weather after a few days respite. The bad weather did not make for comfort, but if it helped to protect us from attack we could certainly put up with it.

The reason for the absence of the U-boats is explained by an entry in Dönitz's War Diary for the day noted:

It therefore looks as though two groups had joined up in the afternoon while up to date very little had been reported about escort, and also no air patrol seemed to be present, suddenly from 1800 onwards all boats were driven off by heavy air activity and large destroyer escort. A number of boats reported aircraft contacts.

As rest of convoy route lay more and more within range of enemy air support, operation was broken off at daylight on 1.11 in CF 69 (315 miles due west of Lisbon).

In a tough four day battle with convoy under favourable weather conditions and not too strong an escort seven boats out of strong group of ten attacked successfully and sank a total of eighteen ships together 133,131 GRT without a single loss.

With the arrival of long-range Liberators of RAF Coastal Command over the convoy on the afternoon of the 31st, and eight more escort vessels in the days following, Admiral Dönitz was wise to withdraw his U-boats. No doubt on the strength of the reports he had received of eighteen ships sunk he was content to do so, satisfied that a significant victory had been gained. As was not unusual, the claims made by the *Streitaxt* Group were inflated, but even so, SL 125 in losing twelve ships totalling 80,005 tons had suffered the greatest loss of any Freetown–UK convoy to date. And the story did not end there. Two months later, eleven of the ships that survived the battle for SL 125 sailed in the westbound convoy ONS 154, bound from Liverpool to New York. This convoy of fifty merchantmen, escorted by a destroyer, five corvettes and a French-manned Special Service Vessel carrying two reconnaissance aircraft, was attacked in mid-Atlantic by a force of twenty U-boats. Thirteen merchant ships and the Special Service Vessel were sunk, among them the British merchantmen *King Edward*, *Lynton Grange*, *Ville de Rouen* and *Zarian*, all of whom had endured and survived the attack on SL 125.

Conclusions

Operation Torch was a resounding success, resulting in the seizure of French North Africa, which then acted as a jumping off ground for the return of the Allies to continental Europe by the back door of Sicily and Italy. This was as planned, but it was beyond the wildest dreams of the planners that 70,000 fighting men, British and American, would be transported across thousands of miles of open ocean without losing one single man to enemy action on the way. It seems to be beyond the bounds of belief that the Germans, with their vast intelligence gathering network, were not aware of what was afoot. So, was there another factor involved?

The great seaborne enterprise code-named Operation Torch began at dawn on 2 October 1942 with a trickle of ships sailing from the Firth of Clyde. Convoy KX 1, the curtain-raiser of Torch, consisted of just five supply ships escorted by three corvettes and five armed trawlers; not a sight to set any U-boat commander's pulse racing. But over the weeks that followed, that insignificant trickle became a flood, with hundreds of ships packed with troops and their equipment flowing southwards from Britain and eastwards from America, all bound for the landing beaches of French North Africa.

Throughout the month of October, and into November, the North Atlantic was thick with the most inviting targets Admiral Dönitz's U-boats could ever hope to see through their watching periscopes. A worried Naval Staff had already warned Admiral Cunningham, C-in-C of all naval forces for Torch, that 'if the enemy got wind of our intentions fifty U-boats could be immediately employed against the expedition.' And yet not one of these ships, said to be 600 in number, so much as 'smelled the powder'. Not one shell, bomb or torpedo came their way whilst on passage. Could it be just coincidence that, at the same time as three convoys unconnected with Torch, RB 1, SC 107 and SL 125, came under heavy and sustained attack, keeping a force of at least forty U-boats occupied, the troop convoys sailed past unnoticed?

In his memoirs, Winston Churchill wrote: 'Our great armadas were approaching the scene. We were determined to spare nothing to safeguard their passage.' What did Churchill mean by 'spare nothing'? An analysis of all the evidence available points to the conclusion that, either deliberately, or as a matter of opportunity, the three convoys described in detail in this book were used as decoys to draw the U-boats away from the Torch convoys.

With regard to Convoy RB 1, what military strategist in his right mind would have sent eight ageing, flat-bottomed, short-haul excursion steamers across a Western Ocean crawling with U-boats, and at the change of the equinox? Furthermore, ancient though they were, by nature of their previous occupation all these ships were capable of speeds in excess of 12 knots, two of them, in fact, the *Boston* and *New York*, being 19-knotters. So why, for much of the time, were they trailing their coats across the wide ocean at 9 knots?

When RB 1 sailed from New York, the preliminaries for Torch were already under way, with thousands of US servicemen being shipped across the Atlantic by fast AT convoys taking a more southerly route. Commencing in January 1942, these were one- or two-ship convoys of fast passenger liners pressed into service as troopships, including the Cunarders *Queen Mary* and *Queen Elizabeth*, with a cruiser escort. It was said that one of these troop convoys was crossing at the same time as RB 1, but there is no record to confirm this in British or American archives.

Many years after the war, Thomas Cottam, Second Officer of the *Northland*, wrote:

> The German side of the story indicates that at the time they certainly believed that we were a troop-carrying convoy; so important in fact that after we had broken through the first patrol, less the Boston and New York, they called in a second pack that was operating to the north to intercept us, which they did on 24th/25th. It always seemed to me that there was a delicate leakage of information and at the same time cover up, to make the RB 1 something other than what it really was. There was a rumour that the real convoy was further to the south.

Convoy SC 107, although carrying mainly war materials, was bound direct for the United Kingdom, and would have expected the U-boats to pounce at some time during the crossing, but not in such numbers and with such ferocity. However, while there is no hard evidence to indicate that this convoy was used as a decoy to draw the U-boats away from UGF 1, it surely cannot be just luck of the draw that led to one convoy being savaged, while the other, a far more crucial body of ships upon which the initial success of Torch depended, passed by unnoticed. Admittedly, the American convoy was very heavily defended, but such odds had not been known to deter the U-boats in the past.

It has since been revealed that it was known as early as August 1942 that Naval Cipher 3, which was used to pass messages between the Admiralty and Washington, had been penetrated by German Intelligence. For some unexplained reason the Admiralty continued to use this code until June 1943. That being so, when SC 107 was on passage all traffic concerning the convoy was being read by *B-Dienst* and passed to the waiting U-boats. In fact, *B-Dienst* had decrypted a British radio message giving comprehensive details of the convoy and its projected route within hours of it sailing. Armed with this knowledge, Group *Veilchen* was able to set up an ambush and completely overwhelm SC 107's weak and inexperienced Canadian escort, resulting in fifteen ships, 100,000 tons of cargo and 150 men being lost. And while SC 107 was under attack, not a million miles away to the south the huge Casablanca-bound Torch convoy UGF 1 with 35,000 troops and their equipment passed by apparently undetected.

SL 125, bound from Freetown to the United Kingdom, had even less relevance to Operation Torch. This was a routine trade convoy; thirty-eight ships carrying the most innocuous of cargoes; beef from the Argentina, tea from India, palm oil from West Africa. With an escort of four corvettes, this convoy had the great misfortune – or so official sources would have it – to be winding its slow way north as, just over the horizon, the highly vulnerable troop carriers of Operation Torch were converging on Morocco. And so, like it or not, SL 125 became a decoy, attracting the attention of Dönitz's U-boats, of which as many as forty, German and Italian, were already on station between the Azores and the Canary Islands.

The German Naval Staff was aware that something big was afoot, but had no idea that the Allies were about to invade French North Africa. Fregattenkapitän Günther Hessler, Dönitz's son-in law, who was on the Staff at the time, summed up the situation:

The Torch landings in November 1942 came as a complete surprise to the Supreme Command. The German Naval Staff assessment was that Allied shipping was being concentrated for a major supply run to Malta and that Allied strength was insufficient to make a North African landing without undue risk. In consequence, U-boat dispositions remained unaltered until far too late, the Atlantic U-boats were far too distant to intervene and support was limited to boats from the Biscay ports. Furthermore, when U-boats intercepted Convoy SL 125 in October 1942, the British realised that others would be attracted away from the route of the Torch convoys.

Influenced by false information spread by British agents, the German Naval Staff came to the conclusion that the Allies were about to make another attempt to take the Vichy French naval base of Dakar, in Senegal, 1,300 miles to the south. With this in mind, Dönitz had gathered together as many U-boats as were available in the area, and stationed them north of the Canaries, ready to intervene. When the ships of SL 125 were sighted south of Dakar, and heading north, it was wrongly assumed that they were an invasion fleet.

Lieutenant John Holm, commanding the corvette HMS *Crocus*, escorting SL 125, wrote in later life:

> We had run into the middle of the U-boat packs waiting around or on their way to Dakar for an expected invasion of that part of Africa. The fact that the enemy had picked the wrong target was unknown to us at the time, though we surely knew they were with us in numbers. Perhaps it was poor consolation to the Germans that what they encountered was a convoy of medium-sized ships heading north when they expected some of the finest ships of the merchant navies of Britain and the US coming from the other direction. This effective though unplanned decoy had another good aspect for the Allies. It kept them adequately in the picture regarding the whereabouts of most of the U-boats in the area and enabled them to direct troop transports and supply ships away from the trouble. We in the convoy were not feeling so elated about the state of affairs. We were not to know that our misfortune helped one of the great invasions in history and perhaps the turning point of the Second World War.

It is worthy of note that the ship chosen to carry the Commodore of SL 125, Rear Admiral Cecil Reyne, was P&O's *Nagpore*, a ship so old and worn out that she could only manage 7½ knots with a fair wind. She was the slowest ship in the convoy, and so dictated the speed of the others. Even submerged U-boats could easily keep pace with

SL 125, and in consequence the convoy lost twelve ships and 407 men. Admiral Reyne, who almost lost his life when the *Nagpore* was torpedoed was moved to comment when it was all over: 'This is the only time I have been congratulated for losing ships.' What exactly did he mean?

It is most unlikely that it will ever be known whether the three convoys, RB 1, SC 107 and SL 125, were offered up as sacrificial lambs to protect the Torch convoys – and now, after so many years have gone by, who will care? Already, the names of those 792 men who died in the decoy convoys have been forgotten. Let this book be a memorial to them.

Bibliography

Blair, Clay, *Hitler's U-boat War: The Hunted 1942–45*, Random House USA, 1999.

Bryant, Arthur, *The Turn of the Tide*, Collins, 1957.

Boutilier, James A., *The RCN in Retrospect 1910–1968*, UBC Press, 1982.

Brown, Anthony Cave, *Bodyguard of Lies*, W.H. Allen, 1976.

Burn, Alan, *The Fighting Commodores: Convoy Commanders in the Second World War*, Pen & Sword, 1996.

Carruthers, Bob, *The U-boat War in the Atlantic, Vol. II, 1942–1943*, Pen & Sword, 2013.

Central Office of Information, *The Battle of the Atlantic*, HMSO, 1946.

Churchill, Winston S., *The Second World War, Vols II, III & IV*, Cassell, 1951.

Costello, John and Terry Hughes, *The Battle of the Atlantic*, Collins, 1977.

Falls, Cyril, *The Second World War*, Methuen, 1948.

Gretton, Sir Peter, *Convoy Escort Commander*, Cassell, 1964.

Hadley, Michael L., *U-boats Against Canada*, McGill-Queen's University Press, 1985.

Haldane, R.A., *The Hidden War*, Robert Hale, 1978.

Holm, John, *No Place to Linger*, Holmwork Publishers Ltd, 1985.

Lamb, James B., *The Corvette Navy*, Macmillan of Canada.

Lavery, Brian, *In Which They Served*, Conway Maritime Press, 2008.

Ministry of War Transport, *Merchantmen at War*, HMSO, 1944.

Moore, Captain Arthur R., *A Careless Word, a Needless Sinking*, Granite Hill Corp., 1983.

Morgan, Daniel and Bruce Taylor, *U-boat Attack Logs*, Seaforth Press, 2011.

Reed, James H., *Convoy 'Maniac' – R.B.1*, The Book Guild, 2000.

Rohwer, Jürgen, *Axis Submarine Successes 1939-1945*, Patrick Stephens, 1983.

Showell, J.P. Mallmann, *U-boats Under the Swastika*, Ian Allan, 1973.

Slader, John, *The Fourth Service*, Robert Hale, 1994.

Smith, Waldo E.L., *The Navy Chaplain and His Parish*, Queens Printer, 1967.

Sproule, Anna, *Port Out Starboard Home*, Blandford Press, 1978.

Stern, Robert C., *Type VII U-boats*, Arms and Armour Press, 1991.

Terraine, John, *Business in Great Waters*, Leo Cooper, 1989.

Thomas, David A., *The Atlantic Star 1939–1945*, W.H. Allen, 1990.

Turner, John Frayn, *Fight for the Sea*, Pen & Sword, 2013.

Walling, Michael G., *Bloodstained Sea*, Cutter Publishing, 2009.

Woodman, Richard, *The Real Cruel Sea*, John Murray, 2004.

Other Sources

National Archives, Kew

Imperial War Museum

www.uboat.net

www.uboatarchive.net

www.naval-history.net

Index